PRAISE FOR ORGANIZATIONAL TRAUMA AND HEALING

Organizational Trauma and Healing is a straightforward and worthwhile read for any non-profit leader who seeks to better understand the complex, nuanced and, sometimes, predictable patterns of organizational behavior and culture. Anyone who works in a non-profit setting – with all of its challenges and enormously deep rewards – will connect with the lessons learned by the authors. This book confirmed my belief that organizations, as well as the individuals within them, need our compassion. While it illuminates struggle, it also offers the insight and hope that every non-profit deserves.

Nan Stoops, Executive Director, Washington State Coalition Against Domestic Violence

Vivian and Hormann have created an important work that will resonate with all those who work in and lead organizations. Their work around organizational trauma creates a language for understanding why certain patterns persist within group life and how these wounds can restrict our capacity to move forward in our work. At iLEAP we work with community leaders from around the world who have used the organizational trauma framework to better understand their work culture and, most important, initiate healing and community building.

Britt Yamamoto, Ph.D., M.S., Executive Director, iLEAP

Organizational Trauma and Healing is a timely and urgently needed book. It is the fruit of decades of individual organizational consulting by the co-authors, and of their collaboration since 1998. Although their focus is on highly mission-driven non-profit organizations, much of what they say is applicable to understanding and consulting with for-profit corporations, and for understanding our wider culture. There are few workplaces today that are untouched by organization-wide trauma, whether as individual events or sustained over a long period of time.

As I was reading their book, I couldn't put it down. It reads like a novel, but one grounded in stories of real, emotionally turbulent, workplace life. Vivian and Hormann develop their methods and models "in the trenches" of their consulting experience. In a sense they are action researchers. They write from the ground up, not from some detached safe place. In their consulting they discuss the undiscussible, address powerful feelings as organizational facts. They paint the long shadow cast by organizational trauma that leaders and employees make into secrets and taboos in order to return the workplace to some fictional "normal."

They repeatedly draw attention to the fact that members of non-profit organizations who deal with traumatized clients themselves insidiously become traumatized from witnessing and internalizing the catastrophic stories. Vivian and Hormann describe the emotionally demanding work of consulting with traumatized organizations, and the importance of self-care and connectedness among the consultants themselves.

As I read their book I asked myself: Who should read this book? My answer is: anyone who has been affected by relentless organizational change over the past thirty years – whether through physical or symbolic violence, whether individual or group. This is a very important book of and for our times.

Howard F. Stein, Ph.D., Professor Emeritus, Department of Family and Preventive Medicine, University of Oklahoma Health Sciences Center, organizational consultant and author of several books on organizational culture including Beneath the Crust of Culture

Organizational Trauma and Healing is a "must read" for heads of non-profits, schools, helping professions, and public service agencies who need to anticipate exposure to traumatic events. Military, veterans, police, and other government leaders will find invaluable insights in helping their organizations avoid and persevere through predictable and random adversity. The authors offer many clear cut "lessons learned" for proactive leaders.

Mark C. Russell, Ph.D., ABPP, U.S. Navy Commander (Retired), Director, Institute of War Stress Injuries and Social Justice, Antioch University Seattle

While reading this book I found myself saying, 'Oh so that's what was going on!" I could definitely relate to the examples and stories and even avoid pitfalls because of what I read. I think this book can help us move from stress and fatigue on the edge of giving up, toward insightful solutions for the health and sustainability of our organizations and ourselves. In this era of rapidly changing environments this is a valuable read!

Cheryl Bozarth, M.A., NCC, Executive Director, Domestic Abuse Women's Network

What lurks in the shadows of traumatized, mission-driven organizations? What are potential negative organizational consequences of social idealism? How do we avoid "catching the disease" we are treating? Vivian and Hormann pose new questions and provide intriguing answers. Years of experience and field research resulted in this practical book. The book's many stories make it more understandable, useful, and convincing. Vivian and Hormann call the devils out of the darkness while lighting the path to performance and health.

Vivian and Hormann help you make sense of the organizational craziness that surrounds you. They set about creating a structure of renewed hope for nonprofits suffering from trauma. They are to be commended for defining organizational trauma. They name it and gain power over it in the process. Leaders troubled by patterns of criticism from within their organizations will find important clues in this book. Perhaps the problems you are experiencing with a few staff members are signs of something larger going on...something that is more about the organization than a few people within it.

Organizations of all types experience trauma. While Vivian and Hormann confine their research to nonprofits, their conclusions reach far beyond that world. Leaders of businesses will find better guidance here than in much of their typical corporate reading.

Geoff Bellman, recognized thought leader on organizations, leadership, life, and change, and author of a number of books on consulting, including Extraordinary Groups, which he coauthored with Kathleen Ryan

As I read this book, I felt the work of twenty plus years of mission driven advocacy work coming into focus, as if a weight is lifting. Each page is a gift and a map for anyone called to serve in an organization addressing the challenging continuum of caring for individual and community needs. Take up this book and use it every day!

Anne Liske, Sexual violence prevention advocate

ORGANIZATIONAL TRAUMA AND HEALING

Pat Vivian and Shana Hormann

DEDICATION

This book is dedicated to those who work in highly mission-driven nonprofit agencies and those who support them.

CONTENTS

ACKNOWLEDGMENTS

This book is the product of our work as consultants, practitioners, and educators, and we are grateful to the many, many people whose paths we have crossed. We owe a huge debt to our clients. Leaders opened their organizations and themselves to our help. They trusted us with their stories and vulnerabilities and worked with us as we developed our thinking and ideas. We would never have been able to write this book without them. Though we are not naming you, you know who you are.

In particular Pat owes an enormous thanks to Kate Rowe-Maloret and her staff at Connections for their honesty and spirit of learning.

Shana wishes to thank the leaders that she interviewed in her Ph.D. research. In particular she is grateful to the two women who inspired the "Dee" and "Cora" stories. Pat and Shana also wish to appreciate the dozens of individuals from Save Our Youth and the rape crisis center who spent hours sharing their experiences. They added an important depth to our understanding and analysis.

Our graduate students at Antioch University Seattle added to the value of our ideas by sharing their experiences about organizational trauma and by applying our ideas in ways that broadened our conceptual framework. In particular, Sarah Murphy-Kangas pushed our thinking by applying our ideas to her work with youth serving agencies, and Kristin (Gray) Cox applied our ideas to her role with the US Coast Guard.

So many colleagues listened to us, challenged us, thought with us, encouraged us, and provided us with opportunities to share our thinking. Many thanks to Howard F. Stein whose friendship, support, and intellectual guidance have enlivened our work and also our deep appreciation for his own research, consulting, and writing about trauma. We also want to thank Bev Emery and the staff at Office of Crime Victim's Advocacy, Judy Chen and Nan Stoops from the Washington Coalition Against Domestic Violence, Gayle Stringer, Mayet Dalila, Jennifer Evans, Lydia Guy, Ann Liske, Stacy Kitchen, Barbara Green, Karen Anderson, Glenda Chaffin, Raquel Gutierrez, Lisa Kreeger, Betsy Grava, and staff at Washington Coalition of Sexual Assault Programs, especially Christi Hurt and Suzanne Brown-McBride. Antioch University faculty and staff colleagues offered constant support and encouragement. They include Professors Mark Hower, Carolyn Kenny, Jon Wergin, Laurien Alexandre, Barbara Spraker, and Peter Rojcewicz.

Most especially we offer profound thanks to Ann McGettigan and Geoff Bellman. From our earliest conversations they took our ideas seriously, encouraged us to develop them, and supported us in that process. In particular we owe Ann a debt of gratitude for her willingness to talk openly about her experiences in nonprofit agencies. Geoff spent hours listening to us and offered essential advice about authoring and publishing a book. He also put us in touch with colleagues in the publishing world who provided feedback and support.

Three individuals acted as editors in this effort. We offer a huge thank you to Kristine Quade and Sarah Murphy-Kangas for several rounds of editing, and to Ginger Rebstock for her careful reading of our final manuscript draft.

We each have champions in our families who made it possible to devote our time and energy to this book. Pat is indebted to her partner, Ginger Rebstock, for many hours of listening and to her daughter – and valued professional colleague – Liz and to her son Matt for their ongoing support and encouragement. Shana's mother, LaReine, and son, Devin, shared their love and were the best cheering section throughout.

Finally, thank you to everyone who kept asking, "When are you going to write a book about organizational trauma?"

1

INTRODUCTION

A stranger walked into an organization that provided women's healthcare services and shot and killed two staff members and wounded others. No one could imagine anything worse. This tragedy left the organization devastated and very vulnerable. Over many months of conversation among co-workers, board members, and peer organizations and consulting with local police the organization regained its footing, but it was changed forever. It recovered from the immediate aftermath of that tragedy, but subsequently the organization acted with an enduring sense of danger and a need to protect itself and "stand strong". The organization built and moved into a new building a few years after this awful event. This new building had an entrance with a metal detector and two armed guards who looked out through bulletproof windows. The guards confirmed that visitors actually had appointments before unlocking the front door. Despite this increased security, the shootings were never far from anyone's consciousness, and staff did not relax. This organization never returned to normal. One staff member reported that:

> When I got into the office the tension was in my body.
> I went to work and did what I needed to do. I felt like it
> never went away.

An intern at the agency years after the attack said that she could feel and sense the threat:

> Though the shootings are never mentioned, the reality
> of them is below the surface at every moment.

Organizational trauma is painful, and its impacts can be catastrophic. Our colleague Howard Stein (personal communication, 9/28/04), who has written extensively about organizations and communities in trauma, describes the phenomenon of collective trauma:

> At any level, trauma is an experience for which a
> person, family, or group is emotionally and cognitively
> unprepared, an experience that overwhelms the self-
> protective structure and leaves the person, family,
> or group feeling totally vulnerable and at least
> temporarily helpless

Trauma and traumatization may result from a single devastating event, from the effects of many deleterious events, or from the impact of cumulative trauma that comes from the nature of the organization's work. Whatever the source, organizations are severely wounded — dealt a lasting collective emotional and psychological blow, seriously hurt in the moment and significantly harmed for the future. The trauma and traumatization overpower the organization's cultural structure and processes and weaken the organization's ability to respond to internal and external challenges.

We have witnessed the harm and pain from traumatic events and from insidious patterns of cumulative trauma. We have heard the poignant stories of individuals who blamed themselves because they and their organizations were devastated by events and patterns that they did not understand and could not control. We know of several organizations that died as a result of traumatization.

Our purpose in writing this book is to strengthen highly mission-driven nonprofit organizations. Our intention is to help leaders and members to understand organizational identity, culture, trauma, and traumatization so they can use that information to heal their organizations and promote organizational health. We define "highly mission-driven nonprofits" as entities with intense and compelling purposes that drive not only organizational goals but also ways in which the work is accomplished. Value-laden language and methods shape the socialization and experiences of the members. These organizations' missions entice individuals to make wholehearted commitments to achieve important and far-reaching changes in society or to help those suffering from societal ills. Examples of compelling missions include:

Table 1.1. Compelling Missions

Mission	Organization
Eliminating Racism Empowering Women	YWCA
To build better lives for the millions of Americans affected by mental illness	National Alliance on Mental Illness

In order to accomplish our purpose we offer a conceptual framework of organizational trauma, practical interventions to address trauma and traumatization, and multiple examples from our professional practices. This book is intended for individuals who work in, lead, fund, and consult with nonprofits. Professionals who work in businesses or corporations outside the nonprofit world may also find our ideas relevant. However, our experiences are primarily with nonprofits so we have focused our expertise and thinking on the dynamics within this sector. In the remainder of this chapter we tell about the progression of our ideas and research and let you the reader know what you can expect in the rest of the book.

The Progression of Our Ideas

Our focused work on understanding and working with traumatized organizations began in 1998. Previously Shana had worked internally as a leader in higher education, nonprofit agencies, and with tribal communities. Pat had spent decades consulting to nonprofits and government agencies. The two of us had been meeting regularly to discuss organizational dynamics and culture with the intention of trying to understand patterns that kept occurring in our work.

From the beginning we approached understanding these dynamics from a system-wide perspective rather than looking at individuals and their behavior. (See Table 1.2.) We knew that in many nonprofits change approaches centered on shifting individual behaviors and using methods such as training to support that approach. We were convinced that this strategy was limited and sought ways to understand a nonprofit as a complete organization so that we could develop ways to help the whole entity. We realized that as long as the focus was on individual behavior, expectations were high for individual staff to change while organizational norms and structure were left untouched. This dynamic fueled a cycle of dissatisfaction and worker and leader turnover. Individuals came and went, but organizational patterns persisted and were left unaddressed. In fact in many cases the patterns were not even perceived. We began to differentiate the impact of a focus on organizations from that of a focus on individuals.

Table 1.2. Individual and Organizational Focus

Focus on Individual	Focus on Organization
Problem identification and problem-solving	Pattern identification and normalization
Individual responsibility	Collective responsibility
Limited impact on sustainability of the organization	Widespread impact on structures, systems, and values
Acceptance of an individual's dysfunctional behavior by the organization	Aspiration to focus on organizational strengths and the central spirit of the work
Understanding the individual leads to the expectation that the individual needs to change	Understanding the whole leads to the expectation that system-wide dynamics need to change

In our practices as consultants and managers we noticed that the kind of work done by an organization seemed to influence its style, values, norms, and ways of operating – its organizational culture (see Table 1.3). For example, in advocacy organizations we witnessed staff "advocating" in their everyday communication with co-workers, supervisors, and board members. They approached these interactions with a sense of urgency, an aggressive posture, and an emphasis on strong convincing techniques. Similarly crisis agencies had trouble creating and maintaining routine structures. Because of sensitivity to crisis and a comfort in handling situations in that manner, they developed what is termed a "crisis mentality". Furthermore, victim services' staff when in conflict with managers and co-workers often framed their issues in terms of power dynamics.

Table 1.3. Impact of Mission/Work of Organization on Organizational Culture

Mission/Work of Organization	Organizational Culture
Advocate on behalf of underserved populations	Communication patterns reflect adversarial influencing strategies rather than collaboration
Provide counseling and support for people in crisis	Processes geared towards crisis response rather than routines and planning
Provide services for victims	Agency personnel believe they are victimized by those who have more power than they do

We also knew that people were drawn to the work of a particular organization for many reasons. The relationships that develop among the main aspects of organizational life – individual, work, and culture – are mutually reinforcing. That mutual reinforcement, together with the nature of highly mission-driven entities, generates and maintains an intense intellectual and emotional atmosphere. In a positive way this reinforcing triangle helps the organization stay true to its mission and solidify the rapport and bonds of its members. In a less productive way this intensity and mutual reinforcement are vehicles for transmission of trauma into the organization and among its members. Figure 1.1 depicts the interplay between the work, the culture and the individuals in the organization.

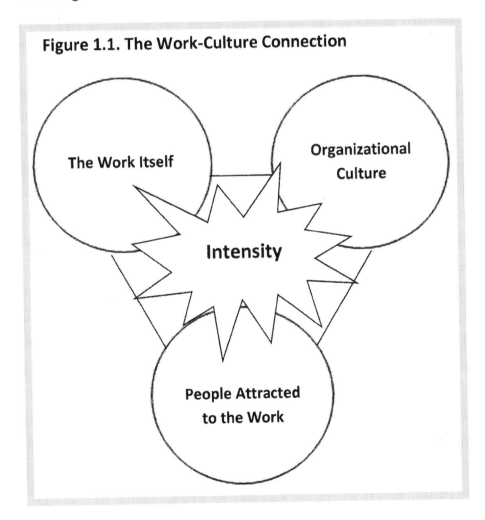

Figure 1.1. The Work-Culture Connection

The Work Itself

Organizational Culture

Intensity

People Attracted to the Work

In the summer of 1999 Pat was asked by the board of directors of a community-based nonprofit to conduct an extensive organizational assessment because the organization had lost its executive director after a tenure of only six weeks. Pat conducted interviews with staff, board, and community members and when she analyzed the data, she began to suspect that the organization was suffering from trauma. She saw organizational patterns – low energy, attitudes of helplessness and hopelessness, and defensive protectiveness – and heard comments that suggested strong organizational parallels to the experiences of individuals who suffered from trauma. Still it was hard for her to imagine that a whole organization might be traumatized at its core. That same summer a local rape crisis center closed its doors. We were dismayed and then puzzled to hear that this agency, which had been a leader in the anti-rape movement since 1972, was gone. We were very familiar with the agency and its work but had not heard anything about agency troubles. We wondered how its demise had happened without our awareness and why it had shut its doors.

As we considered these two organizational stories together, we began to see patterns. We had already come to appreciate the influence an organization's work had on its culture. We suspected that these organizations' particular work with victims of trauma and the subsequent influence of that work on their organizational cultures were contributing to the organizations themselves becoming traumatized systems. The organizations' cultures were becoming collective reservoirs of unhealed trauma. Our work on understanding the connection of an organization's work to its organizational culture and our beginning attempts to conceptualize organizational trauma had come together.

Once we made the connection between work, culture, and trauma, we searched for information and resources about the phenomenon of organizational trauma but could find nothing that referred directly to traumatized systems. We then began to build our own concepts. We shared our ideas with colleagues who worked in nonprofit agencies. We heard similar responses over and over.

My organization was a crazy place to work. I felt bad leaving, but the organization had become so dysfunctional I did not know what else to do.

Your ideas make so much sense to me, and they help me make sense of my previous job.

I had no words for what I was experiencing and no skills to deal with the depth of the situation's dynamics. I wish I had known about organizational trauma back then.

Our ideas seemed to touch a set of painful and little understood experiences.

As we sought to understand how an entity could be traumatized – and the importance of recognizing that possibility – we began to combine concepts and models from the two fields of trauma work with individuals and organization development. We utilized concepts and frameworks from clinical practice, organizational culture, and nonprofit lifecycles to develop an integrated understanding and approach.

We also conducted field research into various dimensions of organizational trauma. As we reflected on that research and our practice experiences, we deepened our understanding of how the work-culture connection could lead to organizational trauma. For example, in agencies providing services to individuals, families, and communities suffering from trauma, the organizational policies, procedures, communication patterns, and daily interactions are conducted with elevated awareness of the gravity of the work. Every aspect of the work is crucial and essential and must be accomplished in the right way. The organizational values and the way the work is done enable the experiences of clients' trauma to enter the organization and become embedded in the organizational culture.

We also realized that organizations could be traumatized from a single devastating event, for example a clinic bombing, or from a pattern of internal or external wounding, such as workplace abuse or ongoing harassment of a religious group, not just the cumulative effects of the work-culture connection. We created a conceptual framework that accounted for these different types of trauma and began to describe the phenomenon of a traumatized system. We also developed strategies for healing traumatized organizations. This book is an important benchmark in our efforts to communicate our ideas about organizational trauma and healing.

The Chapters in This Book

The book is divided into three sections. Part One offers a definition and set of frameworks, historical and conceptual, for understanding organizational trauma and the dynamics associated with its occurrence. Each chapter contains examples from our own practices or a vignette that exemplifies the chapter's concepts. We chose pseudonyms for some organizations to protect the anonymity of the organizations and the individuals with whom we spoke. We indicate when we have used a pseudonym.

Chapter Two describes organizational trauma and places the concept of organizational trauma in disciplinary context. Different types and sources of trauma and traumatization are explored. Chapter Three illustrates ways that the work of an organization influences its culture and describes the function of organizational culture. These ideas help explain the ways an organization might be exposed to traumatic events. Chapter Four examines factors of susceptibility to trauma and describes the syndrome of a traumatized system. Chapter Five tells the story of a rape crisis center's closure highlighting organizational culture; cumulative trauma from services to survivors and social change efforts; two unhealed traumatic events related to leaders leaving; and a cascading series of re-traumatizing events.

Part Two addresses intervention in traumatized organizations and prevention of traumatization in organizations susceptible to it. Chapter

Six focuses on recovery from the immediate aftermath of a traumatic event, including important first steps to stabilize and make sense of the experience as well as longer-term strategies to regain normal functioning. Chapter Seven describes strategies to surface and address unacknowledged trauma, build the organization's health, and reduce susceptibility to more serious traumatization. Chapter Eight focuses on attention to internal patterns and developing ways to strengthen organizational health. We offer our "Strengths and Shadows Model" as a specific technique for paying attention to organizational culture.

Part Three focuses on leader and consultant roles in situations of organizational trauma and traumatization. Chapter Nine describes how leaders influence organizational culture and can help a traumatized organization heal. It illustrates the importance of leadership behavior and modeling in circumstances of trauma and traumatization. Chapter Ten describes the additional perspective and help that can be given by external consultants. It describes the role of consultants in terms of personal and professional qualities, skills, and experience. Chapter Eleven, the conclusion, leaves the reader with final integrating thoughts and ideas for future research and practice.

2

DISCIPLINARY FOUNDATION, FRAMEWORKS, AND TYPOLOGY

This chapter places the concept of organizational trauma in a disciplinary context by relating it to other frameworks describing trauma in individuals and explaining dynamics in organizations. It then offers a typology of the different types and sources of trauma with multiple examples. We start with additional examples of traumatization.

As the story in the introductory chapter shows, a catastrophic event can devastate coping systems that normally provide a sense of control for the organization and its members. These events overwhelm the whole organization and are impossible to ignore. Coping systems fail, and healing from these traumatic events is difficult – sometimes impossible. The organization's people and culture suffer.

Organizations can also be traumatized in less obvious ways. Traumatization can come from repeated wounding actions or the deleterious effects of the organization's work. Because these impacts are not readily noticed, organizations often do not recognize and address them in a timely way. The impacts of these ongoing patterns almost always result in the system becoming traumatized. The following examples describe the impact of cumulative trauma due to wounding actions and the nature of the organization's work.

This first example shows the damage from wounding actions that occurred inside the organization. Linda had just been promoted from her advocate position to be the new executive director of a rural domestic violence services agency. The agency had been poorly managed, with no record keeping and little accountability for public funds. The staff had been badly treated by the previous executive director and subjected to her unethical actions, such as allowing her family members to sleep at the shelter. According to staff, the agency was traumatized during that person's tenure. Because of this troubled history Linda had little idea of normal organizational functioning. The situation was so chaotic she could not make sense of it and felt overwhelmed by her own limitations. Linda knew she could bring constancy and consistency to the agency, but she needed help. She prudently asked for assistance from the executive director of a peer organization. Together they began to bring order and reason to the agency, and the atmosphere improved significantly.

In this second example, the nature of the organization's work led to the trauma. Maureen, executive director of a crisis response agency, felt beleaguered in her leadership role and felt staff hostility aimed at her. She began to believe staff members were trying to push her out of the agency. Maureen was alarmed by her feelings and perceptions and took a deeper look at her organization. She was observing interpersonal conflict among co-workers, and she thought she was seeing evidence of secondary traumatic stress among individual staff members. There was no longer a sense of unity and camaraderie among staff, and she saw the signs of organizational fracturing. Maureen was concerned about the agency's health and services to its clients. When she identified the patterns and realized their seriousness, she sought outside help.

The consultant helped Maureen to frame what was happening in her agency and see there were ways to deal with the dynamics and to heal the organization. As a result of the consultant's assistance the management team became more cohesive, and the executive director and managers learned more about all aspects of secondary traumatic stress. Once they understood the dynamics and the impact on the organization as a whole, Maureen and her team instituted policies and procedures to make resources available for staff members.

Maureen's agency was exhibiting dynamics of intrapersonal and interpersonal stress and conflict that had roots in deeper patterns connected to the nature of its work. The organizational culture was showing some common negative effects from its crisis response work. When she started feeling concerned, Maureen knew to look beneath the interpersonal symptoms for deeper understanding of the situation.

Both examples speak to less obvious traumatization than what occurs from the results of a catastrophic event. In the first story the traumatization came from internal wounding behaviors. In the second story it came from the empathic nature of the organization's work. The examples show the importance of recognizing something is wrong and seeking to understand the urgency and underlying dynamics of the situation.

Disciplinary Foundation of Our Framework

Our disciplinary foundation comes from two bodies of work; the first is clinical practice and research with victims of trauma, first responders, and professionals exposed to others' traumas. The second is organization development practice and theory.

From clinical trauma work we utilized concepts about the profound suffering of victims of trauma and their caregivers to help us understand the intense distress that happens at the organizational level. We translated the post-trauma experience of individuals who had been exposed to traumatic events or had been traumatized themselves into an understanding of the collective dynamics operating in a traumatized system.

From organization development, we used concepts that described the nature and dynamics of whole systems to help us articulate an alternative approach to the more-common focus on individual behavior and actions. Integrating concepts from these two fields provided a way to think about how trauma and traumatization negatively impacted whole entities and what could be done to help those systems heal.

In this next section we describe in detail these foundational concepts and our framework for understanding organizational trauma.

Clinical perspective and concepts

Posttraumatic stress disorder

Posttraumatic Stress Disorder or PTSD is an anxiety disorder that individuals may develop after seeing or living through a dangerous event. These events include violent personal assaults, natural or human-caused disasters, accidents, or military combat. Under usual circumstances an individual in danger has a healthy reaction meant to protect him or her from harm. This is a normal response to the kinds of dangerous events described above. Fear triggers split-second changes in his or her body to prepare to defend against the danger or to avoid it. The person experiences a heightened physical, emotional, and mental state. After the danger has passed, the individual calms down and returns to normal functioning.

Some individuals, for a variety of reasons related to the effectiveness of their coping systems, remain in that heightened state for prolonged periods. This state begins to debilitate their abilities to cope. Individuals suffering from PTSD feel stressed or frightened even when they are not in danger. Many experience helplessness, feelings of confusion, and isolation. They may be continuously hypervigilant, feel extremely anxious, and re-experience the event through nightmares or flashbacks. In an attempt to control their feelings of anxiety they narrow every aspect of their lives including relationships, thoughts, and activities (Herman, 1992).

Table 2.1. Clinical and Organizational Perspectives

Clinical Perspective	Organizational Perspective
Intense individual reactions to traumatic events are normal	Intense organization-wide reactions to traumatic events are normal
Posttraumatic Stress results from an individual's direct experience of trauma and failure to regain previous functioning	Organizational Traumatization results from an organization's experience of trauma and failure to regain previous functioning
Secondary Traumatic Stress results from caring for others who experience trauma	Cumulative trauma becomes embedded in organizational cultures
Susceptibility to PTSD or STS depends on individual history and other factors	Susceptibility depends on organizational history and other factors
Impacts increase with intensity and prolonged period of exposure	Impacts increase with intensity and prolonged period of exposure
Individuals feel anxious, fearful, and helpless	Organizational cultures become anxious and exhibit helplessness
Individuals become hypervigilant and limit exposure to others	Organizations strengthen protective boundaries to limit exposure to outsiders
Helpers may develop STS and compassion fatigue from working with people in trauma	Organizations that value compassion and empathy are exposed to STS and compassion fatigue
Individuals narrow relationships, and activities to control anxiety	Organizations turn inward
Individuals become susceptible to depression and loss of hope	Organizations become susceptible to isolation and despair

We see analogous patterns in organizations. Like a person who suffers from PTSD, the organizational culture becomes hypervigilant and puts up protective boundaries to limit its exposure to outsiders. The culture itself becomes an anxious repository of feelings with an atmosphere of helplessness and isolation. In addition, the organization's patterns of storytelling and rituals act as flashback mechanisms. Not all organizations that suffer from a devastating traumatic event become a traumatized system. Similarly to individuals, some organizations are more susceptible than others to suffering this way. The healthcare organization described in the introductory chapter exhibited some of these characteristics. Table 2.1 summarizes the parallels between clinical and organizational perspectives.

Secondary traumatic stress

Secondary traumatic stress (STS) is a natural response of individuals to caring for or helping those who suffer from trauma. It refers to increased internal stress, negative emotions, distorted mental constructs, and behavior changes that result from being exposed to others' trauma stories. Therapists, family members, first responders, and others who learn about the suffering of clients and loved ones are highly susceptible to STS. The more intense and prolonged the period of exposure to the traumatization of others, the more deleterious are the effects. Compassion stress (Figley, 1995), which comes from using empathy in caring for others who have experienced trauma, ultimately results in the physical, mental, and emotional exhaustion of compassion fatigue. Vicarious traumatization (VT) refers to identity alterations, negative shifts in worldview, and other transformations that occur within therapists as the result of empathic engagement with clients' trauma experiences (Pearlman and Saakvitne, 1995). VT includes strong reactions of grief, rage, and outrage from repeatedly hearing stories of horror that accumulate and grow over time. VT ultimately includes feelings of sorrow, numbness, a deep sense of loss, and loss of hope.

Analogously, organizations as entities are vulnerable to secondary traumatic stress; we use the term "cumulative trauma" to describe this stress. Compassion, frequently an organizational value, and empathy, an organizational resource essential to the provision of care and services, expose the whole entity to secondary traumatic stress. An organization may be exposed to traumatic material through the vehicle of empathy employed by staff to serve clients. As in vicarious traumatization, an event or series of events or influences may cause a shift in organizational worldview that leaves the entity's culture susceptible to isolation and despair. Without intervention or mitigation the organization eventually reaches a state of exhaustion and hopelessness. The rape crisis center mentioned in the introductory chapter showed these signs of exhaustion and hopelessness just before it closed.

Although STS by its various names has been described as the natural outcome of exposure to others' trauma, there are exacerbating factors as well as preventative and mitigating ones. Anyone with unrecognized or unhealed traumas in their personal history may be especially vulnerable to secondary traumatic stress, vicarious traumatization, or compassion fatigue. Individuals without healthy opportunities to recognize and address the impacts they are experiencing run the risk of persistent STS symptoms. For professionals, education about the impact of exposure to others' trauma, clinical supervision, peer support, work-life balance, and rejuvenating activities help mitigate the potentially long-term effects of doing trauma work. For family and community members, a strong support system and specific education about trauma help lessen the negative impacts of being close to someone suffering from trauma.

Similarly at the organizational level, exacerbating and mitigating factors may also exist. Positive aspects of organizational culture, history, worldview, and resources may mitigate any negative impact on the system, resulting in a fairly quick recovery for the system. Conversely, negative aspects of those factors may exacerbate the trauma's impact on the system and result in the system becoming traumatized. As with individuals who have history of personal trauma that goes unrecognized and unhealed, organizations with a history of trauma that goes unrecognized and unhealed may be more susceptible to further traumatization.

Organization Development Perspective

Organizational culture

Organizational culture is the repository of assumptions and beliefs shared by organizational members; those assumptions and beliefs define in a taken-for-granted fashion an organization's view of itself (the internal landscape) and its environment (the external landscape). Culture is clearly evidenced by organizational structures, processes, and espoused values. The organization's unconscious assumptions operate in a less obvious but very powerful way and manifest through the actions and patterns of organizational members.

Comprehending an organization's culture provides a systemic understanding of the multiple layers of organizational life. Understanding the pervasive and enduring nature of organizational culture also serves as a reminder that cultural patterns survive beyond any single person, group, or time period. The concept of organizational culture helps to explain the powerful influences of the work of highly mission-driven nonprofits on organizational life.

For example, many rape crisis centers started in the early to mid-1970s when victims of rape were often not believed and were even blamed for being raped. Rape crisis program rationales described rape as a crime of power. Staff and volunteers were socialized to listen nonjudgmentally to the victim and believe her story, i.e., to think and act differently from the societal norm. Organizational values also encouraged the empowerment of women who had been assaulted and an atmosphere of "by women for women". Over time organizational language shifted from "victim" to "survivor" to further women's empowerment. These ideas, values, and language had an enduring influence on sexual assault service organizations.

Redemptive organizations

A redemptive organization is a type of entity established to benefit society or a disadvantaged or oppressed group. The culture of such organizations is centrally defined by this altruistic purpose. Redemptive organizations (Couto, 1989), seek to redeem society from some evil as well as support the growth of their members. Because of these dual purposes, redemptive organizations are vulnerable to becoming highly sensitized to the ills they are trying to address. Organizational insiders may become overly attentive to internal dynamics and judgmental of how peers live out the organization's values. Staff and volunteers may end up focusing inward because they cannot stand to face the experiences of defeat in the external environment. They try to analyze and fix internally what they cannot fix externally. For example, we heard stories about how co-workers walked on eggshells around each other because they were afraid of being critiqued or judged about their level of passion for the mission and cause.

Stages of nonprofit lifecycle

Nonprofit organizational life follows a developmental process. Organizations are founded with compelling visions and ideas; survive the struggles of the early years of few resources and high excitement; experience growing pains as they become successful and better known; grow into mature entities when they develop sufficient structures and processes to stabilize the organization; and become sustainable if they develop ways to keep abreast of a changing environment. Developmentally speaking, a shift from one stage to another may be challenging. How organizations handle these shifts depends on the organizational culture, leadership, and resources available. Knowledge of the lifecycle itself gives an organization a way to anticipate future changes, both the fact that change will be necessary and the typical developmental tasks called for at each stage. Without this knowledge organizations run the risk of surprise and stress at critical junctures. For example, the charismatic leader who founded an agency and whose vision drew others to the work may not be the leader who is needed at the helm as the organization grows in size and scope. Or informal structures that made the agency feel welcoming and safe may not be strong enough to support a spurt of expansion in programs and staff. Moving through these stages can be a daunting process; sometimes the organization destabilizes into crisis. Weathering that crisis, even under very difficult circumstances, eventually leaves the organization stronger for its next developmental tasks.

In contrast, organizational trauma is not part of the normal organizational lifecycle. It is a disruptive occurrence or pattern outside the usual organizational experience. While nonprofit lifecycle shifts are predictable, organizational trauma by its nature is not. It can and does occur at any stage in an organization's lifecycle. Organizational trauma is not weathered easily and does not necessarily result in a stronger organization. How lifecycle transitions are managed might mitigate or exacerbate an organization's susceptibility to trauma and traumatization. How organizations heal from trauma and mitigate the effects of traumatization in their system influences how successfully they will navigate their lifecycle transitions.

Distinguishing between organizational lifecycle transitions, organizational crises, and organizational trauma is important. Most managers and leaders operate with a limited framework of ideas about organizational dynamics. They interpret what is going on as individual problems or issues or normal nonprofit functioning. Sometimes they recognize situations as organizational crises. Rarely do they see patterns related to organizational trauma. Managers' limited understanding means their inaction or choice of intervention may not fit the circumstances. Detrimental patterns continue.

Using the above disciplinary frameworks related to clinical work with individuals and organization development as well as our experiences as practitioners, we built our framework of understanding about organizational trauma and traumatization. We realized there were many types and sources of trauma and traumatization. (See Table 2.2.) This chapter continues with an exploration of the different types and sources.

Types and Sources of Trauma

There are a variety of ways that organizations might suffer from trauma and end up to be traumatized systems. This section's descriptions and stories act as cautionary tales for nonprofits whose work is empathic or redemptive in nature. And they remind all organizations that they are vulnerable to sudden devastating events and ongoing wounding.

Table 2.2. Types and Sources of Trauma

Type	Source	Examples
Single devastating event	External	Attack on a workplace, loss of funding
Single devastating event	Internal	Suicide of leader, abusive behavior, insider embezzlement
Ongoing wounding	External	Threats or overt hostility directed at organization from community
Ongoing wounding	Internal	Abusive or destructive management practices
Empathic nature of the work	Internal	Unclear boundaries, over-identification with clients
Redemptive nature of the work	Internal	Internalized judgment, guilt, depression, despair

Single devastating events

Single or multiple devastating events harm a wide variety of organizations, groups, and communities. They are society's most visible examples of organizational trauma, though they are not by any means the most common. These events parallel the experiences of individuals who suffer from devastating trauma and develop Posttraumatic Stress Disorder (PTSD). The entity as a whole is disrupted in a profound and destabilizing way. Its defenses are breached, and organizational normalcy is destroyed. Attention to this breach is essential if an organization is going to recognize and address the collective harm it is experiencing.

External devastating events

Events perpetrated by an individual or an entity outside the organization, for example, the bombing of a workplace, burning of a mosque, or the assault or murder of staff, such as the story about the women's healthcare provider recounted in the introductory chapter, happen in front of the whole community and communicate a disdain or hatred for the organization and its identity and values. Tragedies like these are not restricted to highly mission-driven nonprofits. However, when they are perpetrated on highly mission-driven nonprofits, they can shake the foundation of an organization that counts on its community for support. These events can also cause the collapse of an entity already weakened by some other form of trauma.

The following example was a highly publicized tragedy. We include a public trauma in this category in order to show the widespread impact on a community. On April 19, 1995, Timothy McVeigh set off explosives in front of the Alfred P. Murrah Federal Building in downtown Oklahoma City. The explosion tore the building apart and killed 168 people, including 19 small children in the building's daycare center. The surrounding area looked like a war zone and images of the horror spread quickly across the country.

Other single events might be less publicly tragic but are still devastating to the organizations and individuals involved. For example, in the mid-1980s a youth-serving agency had its public funding for emergency shelter beds abruptly pulled. Suddenly the only shelter for runaway youth in the city was shut down. Staff were shocked and protested immediately, but in the meantime everyone scrambled to find safe and stable housing for youth whose lives were already unstable and unsafe.

Internal devastating events

Devastation can also come from inside the organization. Abuse, murder, suicide, or egregious embezzlement rocks the structure and culture of the organization. In addition to the physical harm perpetrated, these events betray the social trust among members and destroy the organization's social fabric. The elements of an organization's culture – factors that keep the organization functioning – are temporarily or permanently destroyed. These events are especially ruinous to organizations with highly visible ideals, values, and goals, since these organizations rely on the trust invested in them because of their reputation and ethics.

For example, a church congregation discovered its pastor had sexually abused women in the congregation. After that pastor left, a new pastor was called to the church. The people in the church did not seem able to accept and trust the new pastor so religious leaders of the denomination's hierarchy were brought in to help this congregation heal. Unfortunately, the destruction of trust between the previous pastor and congregation had fatally destroyed the congregation's spiritual foundation. Even with help it could not recover, and eventually the church disbanded.

Another example: A nonprofit healthcare service provider for lesbian, bisexual and transgendered women served a vulnerable population that had few options for safe and sensitive healthcare. The organization discovered and reported serious embezzlement by its executive director to the police. The organization was left with no money so the board of directors stopped operations and laid off staff. Though the community badly needed these services, no way was found to undo the harm done by the embezzlement. The agency closed permanently and the community lost a vital resource.

A third example: A staff member in a shelter unit of a youth-serving agency sexually assaulted a client. The unit's workers felt traumatized. The organization's management team also felt traumatized because this crime had happened under their leadership. The management team immediately sought help for unit staff to talk through their experiences and feelings. In addition the managers speedily acted to address shortcomings in their policies and procedures to prevent a repeat occurrence. The organization learned from the experience and addressed it in a way that strengthened the organization itself. The organizational memory still contains the event, but it holds little emotional charge, and the organization members seem confident that this kind of tragedy will not happen again.

Devastating events disrupt organizations in obvious ways. When an external source is responsible, the organization's place in the community comes into question. When an internal source is responsible, the event tests an organization's values and structures. Whether from an internal or external source, these events need a strong effective response from organizational leaders and members to deal with the aftermath.

Ongoing wounding

Ongoing wounding – collective emotional and psychological injury that builds over time – can also come from external or internal sources. This type of trauma usually does not rise to the catastrophe of a single event, but nonetheless it disables an organization with an accumulation of harm.

External ongoing wounding

There are several types of external wounding. One is a pattern of unstable, unreliable, and inconsistent financial support. Threats to cut or eliminate funding create economic stress on the organization as a whole and a scary context for staff and clients. Some organizations end up feeling victimized by changing political and social priorities in which certain problems fall out of favor while others are noticed for the first time. Program consistency and effectiveness and future planning are compromised, and the organization as a whole suffers from a lack of confidence in its capacity to take care of itself. For example, a grassroots organization run by and for homeless individuals suffered a precipitous funding cut and was unable to keep its shelter facilities open. Many individuals ended up sleeping on the streets. After months of closure the group's funding was temporally restored. However, the organization remained under a permanent threat of its funding being lost. The organization's security was destroyed.

In many circumstances agencies are placed in competition with peers for limited resources and must make the case that they are more capable of using the money effectively – and therefore more worthy of its receipt. This expectation adds stress to a whole service sector by making natural allies more competitive with each other and leaving all of them more isolated and weak.

For example, a state government decided that it needed to reduce funding for services to victims of crime. As part of that decision it reorganized the manner in which it distributed those funds. Some programs and agencies within designated regions would lose funding while others would survive and need to collaborate or compete with each other for a smaller pool of money.

In another example, a number of agencies in a large metropolitan area provided services to victims of sexual assault. One agency suddenly closed, and a small group of individuals decided to start a new group to serve specific vulnerable populations. This group asked for public money originally designated for the closed agency. Established peer agency leaders lobbied hard against that request and asked that the city redistribute those dollars to their agencies. When the city declined that request and instead agreed to fund the new organization, those peer agencies' leaders started disparaging the new group to various city staff and funders. Staff and volunteers from the new group felt beleaguered, unsupported, and alienated from organizations that might have been close allies.

Sometimes outsiders attack organizations more directly. Detractors question the worthiness of the clients and the integrity of the organization's efforts. In some instances unsympathetic community members use denial of the problem or existing societal prejudice or hostility toward those who are served to erode support for the organization. For example, staff in a rural multi-service program were called "feminazis" by the county prosecuting attorney. The attorney's attitude, noticed in a small community, signaled an attitude of disrespect for staff and lack of support for the work of the program.

Another example: A group of women and men joined together to start an organization to provide services to victims of family violence. In the agency's early months those individuals faced verbal hostility from friends and neighbors and harassment by the wider community. Letters to the editor of the local paper questioned the need for services, the agency's office windows were smashed, and individuals involved were told that they were no longer welcome to shop at the local grocery store. This beginning left a residue of distrust and distance between the agency and the community it served. Some years later that residue made it more difficult for this agency to reach out to the community after a trauma.

When these kinds of wounding occur, the organization learns not to count on outsiders and develops a defensive mentality to protect itself. The organization's culture embraces a perspective that the organization is alone and potentially unsafe in its environment. It also reinforces the definition of insiders as those who can be trusted to understand the importance of the group's efforts. As the organization loses faith in its community, it is cut off from potential supporters and becomes even more isolated in its work. These organizational dynamics mirror those of an individual suffering from PTSD, whose life is narrowed by his or her experience. The organization's functioning is likewise constricted and inhibited.

Internal ongoing wounding

There also exist internal patterns of wounding that may lead to organizational traumatization. These patterns of wounding can come from exploitation of staff, harassment of employees, and workplace abuse. Since these dynamics arise within a supposedly safe atmosphere, their impacts can be even more devastating than the effects of external wounding. Instead of a culture characterized by internal support and care, the culture begins to mirror an uncaring external society. Repeatedly harmful actions unravel the social fabric of the organization; fear pervades the work atmosphere, and trust is destroyed. Staff begin to exhibit distrust of anyone in a leadership role and end up isolating themselves from peers as well. Sooner or later staff act in ways to protect themselves and their jobs, while still trying to serve clients. In some circumstances employees who speak out about what they see happening are targeted for retaliation. Eventually individuals develop a helpless and cynical attitude regarding anything improving, and the culture is defined by fear and hopelessness. Staff turnover increases, newly hired workers are exposed to the same dynamics, and they too learn ways to protect themselves.

Sharon, a newly hired executive director in a small rural agency, described her agency as "broken and totally traumatized. The organization could have died. It was on the brink." Sharon discovered the former executive director had sabotaged staff, projects, and the agency through public embarrassment of staff, threats to employees about job loss, and public pronouncements of poor staff performance. In addition the former executive director had failed to comply with funding requirements from their main funding source, an action that led to the organization's being placed on probation. These behaviors led to an atmosphere of vigilance, fear, and cynicism and a culture of distrust towards leaders. Sharon thought this set of actions gravely damaged the agency and endangered its existence.

Further examples of internal wounding include embezzlement or egregious mismanagement of funds or organizational processes. We have heard many stories in which an incoming leader was faced with an organization in disarray: unacknowledged debts, unpaid bills, unaccounted-for funds, weak or nonexistent infrastructure systems, and no safeguards. These patterns threaten the organization's stability and credibility with external funders and supporters. Though not intentionally abusing or exploiting staff, the patterns also create job insecurity and chaos in programs. When individuals cannot count on consistency and reasonableness, they become protective and cynical.

A rural program in Alaska faced possible disaster when it was discovered that the bookkeeper had been embezzling money from the organization. The embezzlement itself was traumatizing to the organization, "like having your house burgled, it was a violation of trust." However, the more serious trauma came from the way agency leaders handled the situation. The executive director felt a need to contain the information about the embezzlement. As a result some staff felt they were shut out of important conversations and that there were secrets within the organization.

> "The sense of...certain people being considered part
> of the inner circle contributed to a schism within the
> organization..."

That schism negatively affected morale and staff ownership of programs. It took the agency years to heal from this situation.

Even when leadership changes, mismanagement ends, or abusive patterns are stopped, the aftermath of these harmful patterns affects the organization's atmosphere and psyche. The organization sees itself as less capable and effective, and the culture exudes defeat or apathy. Often subsequent leaders find that staff are suspicious and unwilling to invest trust in them or have faith in fair process. Sometimes the harm is so deep that turnaround is impossible and the organization is doomed. The disbanding of the church described earlier in this chapter shows how this could happen.

Cumulative trauma

Many organizations do not experience the situations or dynamics described above. However, they still may face other patterns that lead to traumatization. Harm from repeated exposure to trauma through the organization's work builds up insidiously and exists in the organizational culture as a reservoir of unhealed wounds.

Empathic work

Many highly mission-driven organizations seek to provide services to individuals who have been harmed directly or whose needs have been neglected. In these agencies empathy and compassion form the foundation of approach to someone who is hurt and asking for help. Staff and volunteers are trained directly and socialized indirectly to use empathy in their practice so they are regularly exposed to the pain and suffering of others. Staff who do not work directly with clients are also exposed because they hear stories of truly awful occurrences and dire circumstances from their co-workers. The core identity and worldview of the organization, which frequently include the value of compassion, become inextricably tied up with experiences of trauma and reactions to those experiences.

For example, an organization working with highly vulnerable street youth was known for its commitment to these youth. In emergency situations – phones ringing in the middle of the night or the death of a youth – staff acted with empathy, speed, and unity. When staff focused on the welfare of the youth and their immediate needs, meetings were tension free. However, meetings that addressed the welfare and long-term plans of the agency proved to be a struggle. Betty, the staff person responsible for facilitating the agency's long-term planning process, realized the organization was having trouble focusing on its future. She thought the organization's in-the-moment crisis work might be impacting its ability to think ahead. Betty realized that organizational norms were replicating patterns of interaction with youth in crisis. She finally concluded that addressing the harsh everyday realities of street life was easier than "future talk." As a result of its empathic approach to the street youth the organization had diminished capacity to plan for its own future.

A client of a small anti-domestic violence program was murdered by her husband. The murder shocked everyone and shook the agency to its roots. Previously the agency's perspective had been "some men batter their wives." After the client's death the agency's story shifted to "all men were potential batterers." The agency became more protective of its clients and more wary in its interactions with men. Vicarious traumatization at the organizational level occurred. Organizational VT also affected the agency's relationships with its peer organizations. Agency leaders thought other service providers should have been doing a better job in their work with batterers. As a result of these shifts in worldview, the agency's relationships with other service providers deteriorated, and the agency became more isolated.

Redemptive work

The redemptive work of highly mission-driven nonprofits also can be a source of trauma. Redemptive work – seeking to change society – can stand on its own, for example, in advocacy-based organizations that work on welfare reform or justice for immigrants. Or it can act as a complementary function to empathic work in agencies like rape crisis centers. The organization's core identity includes a strong commitment to social change or social justice. That commitment creates an expectation of struggle for achievement of broad and far-reaching goals to change society. The struggle is fraught with high expectations and high chance of failure. Repeated failures at social change efforts can be disillusioning and disheartening and eventually result in guilt, depression, helplessness, and even despair spreading throughout the organization.

For example, staff members in an agency that served victims of crime were stunned by a not-guilty verdict in a sexual assault trial. After spending hours talking about the sadness and anger they felt about that outcome, staff turned to what they could do. What would be a proactive action? Did they have any power? If they did anything publicly, how would those actions affect the victim? Staff expressed fear about making things worse and worried that no message would be received well. The whole organization felt paralyzed about what action to take. Their paralysis reflected their sense of powerlessness to affect public opinion. The agency's traumatization came from deep feelings of helplessness and hopelessness in making any real change in the community.

Redemptive work can lead to trauma in another way. As noted before, the worldview of an organization is deeply affected by the response of the community to its work. Since the core identity of the organization focuses on changing societal norms and behaviors, a clash of values between the organization and wider society is commonplace. A gap between organizational members' belief in the importance of their work and society's ignorance or denigration of that work reinforces the separation and isolation of the organization from its environment. Community members might respond to organizational efforts with harassment, hostility, and even violence. Some of these instances are devastating or wounding events in and of themselves, but others, while not devastating or wounding, add to the insidious buildup of stress, defensiveness, helplessness, and depression.

In the early 1970s rape crisis center volunteers worked hard to persuade the general public and medical and legal providers of the existence of child sexual abuse. Advocates faced skepticism and denial when they tried to raise awareness about this tragedy. Despite clear evidence of this crime, the community as a whole would or could not accept this reality. The agency felt burdened by its inability to convince the community to protect children.

Finally, redemptive organizations are predisposed to an expectation that insiders "walk the talk" and exemplify values of social change. This underscores the idea that individuals are identifying with a struggle or movement, not simply doing a job. These expectations heighten a sense of internal scrutiny, and sometimes in more dysfunctional situations accelerate a downward spiral of negative dynamics.

For example, an anti-poverty agency saw commitment to anti-racism work as essential to achieving its mission of ending poverty and achieving social justice for all people. As staff became sensitized to the effects of racism on clients, they also became sensitive to these dynamics within the agency. As more discussions focused on internal agency dynamics, many staff reported feeling angry and unsafe in conversations meant to promote learning and dialogue. Instead of resulting in an organization-wide effort to address racism in its many forms, the conversations led to judgments, separation, and polarization among organizational members.

Deleterious effects caused by empathic and redemptive work remind all nonprofits that they can be at risk of traumatization. If leaders and members pay attention to the health of their agency, they lessen the dangers from unaddressed trauma in their culture.

This chapter provided a disciplinary context for our work, a brief description of our conceptual framework for organizational trauma, and a detailed explanation of the types and sources of trauma and traumatization. The effect of the work of an organization on its culture is a central component of our conceptual framework of organizational trauma. In the next chapter we explore this topic and describe instances in which the work itself can expose the organization to traumatization.

3

THE WORK-CULTURE CONNECTION

Highly mission-driven nonprofits develop especially strong cultures, with conscious, visible, and discussed elements as well as unconscious, less visible, and unrecognized elements. In the case of traumatized organizations, more extreme interconnections of work and organizational culture occur. These cultures – healthy and sustainable or unhealthy and traumatized – perform critical functions for members and nonmembers alike. This chapter explores the mechanisms that allow the work to influence an organization's culture and the resulting realities of that influence, including how organizations become traumatized systems. We start with an example that shows the power and dynamics of organizational culture over time.

The Seattle Counseling Service Story

The following example illustrates the interplay of work and culture. Seattle Counseling Service (SCS) began in 1969, making it the oldest mental health agency serving the Lesbian, Gay, Bisexual, Transgendered, and Queer community in the United States. It was established as part of the Dorian Society, which was an organization supporting gay rights. SCS later expanded to become an independent organization serving diverse members of the community, including bisexual, transgendered, and queer-identified individuals.

In the late 1960s a local doctor began talking with individuals who came to him with issues about their sexual identity. Through word of mouth others heard about him and word began to spread in the gay community.

Others joined the doctor in this effort, and in 1969 SCS officially, but not publicly, opened its doors. It began in a rented house, with a telephone and several volunteers, who were ready to answer the phone, talk with people who dropped by, and offer counsel and support.

In the 1960s the wider community viewed gays and lesbians as aberrant. It was an era in which gays and lesbians were harassed, threatened, and physically harmed. Coming out – and being out – during that time were acts of significant bravery in the face of a hostile society. This historical context itself was traumatizing for any group wanting to help lesbians and gay men.

Intending to provide therapy for individuals, Seattle Counseling Service had offices in a secret location. Its location was communicated only by word of mouth. A gasoline can and matches were kept on top of the filing cabinet that held client information so in case of a raid, records that might endanger clients could be burned. For good reasons this agency erected a protective organizational boundary between itself and the wider community. The effects of this initial need for protection and the secrecy it engendered stayed a part of the organization's identity for decades.

Despite dangers from an unsympathetic and hostile environment, from its inception SCS demonstrated its compelling mission of caring for its community and courage to provide services. In SCS's 40th Anniversary Video (YoYoStringmedia.com 2010) an individual commented that SCS founders poured their hearts into the agency and the people who were served. A person who benefited from SCS's help said he learned he did not have to kill himself because he was gay. "I would not have made it without SCS."

In the 1990s, when Seattle was a safer place for the sexual minorities and the LGBT community was more visible and "out", SCS's offices, while not secret, had only modest signage signaling their existence. The agency described itself as rather hidden and separated from the wider community. Staff and board members acknowledged a combination of early agency history and a continuing desire to protect their clients and the LGBT community as influential dynamics in the organization's identity. A combination of internalized homophobia within SCS and a continuing stigma associated with mental illness in the wider community kept staff hesitant about being "out" as an organization. A staff person said, "SCS hid its light under a bushel."

A confluence of events in the early 2000s prompted SCS to change. SCS was asked to take over chemical dependency programs from a peer LGBT community agency that was closing. SCS's agreement to do this prompted organizational soul searching. To serve the breadth of clients in these more complex programs SCS needed to expand its identity. It was time to face the issues of stigmatization and homophobia and to address SCS's cultural fears about being highly visible in the community. SCS had to be a visible healthy model for the community it served. The agency needed to "come out". After many heartfelt conversations about the need for increased visibility and activity in the wider community, SCS decided to expand its mission to be a multi-service resource for the LGBTQ community. It exhibited organizational bravery in coming out.

By the 2000s SCS had grown from a small hidden group of trusted providers to a widely-known, highly-regarded, and frequently-consulted mental health and addiction services agency. Today SCS's eighteen-foot rainbow sign on the side of its building proudly announces its offices. This sign has become a symbol not only of SCS's visibility but also a symbol of LGBTQ pride in Seattle.

SCS began in a dangerous time for the lesbian and gay community. That danger was traumatizing for individuals involved and for the organization as a whole. SCS's story describes the traumatic elements of that beginning: Active community hostility, the dangers of being "out", the fear associated with being a client or a volunteer, and the protective reactions to that fear. SCS's story also shows the persistence over time of early cultural elements that addressed organizational fears – an attitude of "let's not be too open about our work". Its story also demonstrates the power of one organization to overcome its history of trauma and to shift its culture from one influenced by fear and caution to one acting "out and proud" in its environment.

With the SCS story as backdrop, we turn to understanding organizational culture and its relationship to organizational work and trauma. Organizational culture, an expression of the organization's consensual reality, emerges from a complex interplay of natural environment, physical realities, and social interaction. That culture is sustained over time by shared meaning, understanding, and socialization. The power of organizational culture lies in its pervasive and unique nature, one that is conscious and unconscious, obvious and subtle. That nature is embedded in every organizational function and process, and all functions and processes are embedded in the organization's cultural context. Definitions of success, expressed values, dominant leadership styles, language, stories, secrets, and organizational personality make the organization unique.

Work-Culture Connection

In this section we examine specific ways the mission and efforts of highly mission-driven nonprofits influence the cultures of those organizations and how those influences can result in organizational trauma. The work of an organization shapes its culture by:

- Founders' experiences and understanding

- Organizational creation story

- Organizational moral narrative

- Values and standards inherent in the work

- Boundary setting necessary for the work to be credible to its clients and its members

- Identification with wider social change efforts

Though described discretely in this chapter, these aspects build on and reinforce one another. The organization's founding, creation story, and moral narrative come from the early ideas that the founders have about the work that is needed. Defining characteristics of the work and a set of emerging standards and values follow from that foundation. Boundaries emerge from the foundation and the unique characteristics of the work. The boundaries identify who may be served and who may be involved in the effort and define the relationship between the organization and its environment. Identification with broader change efforts emerges from these other aspects.

Founders' experiences and understanding

Highly mission-driven nonprofit organizations start with founders' desires to make a positive difference in their communities. Their desires usually come from personal experiences of being hurt or treated unjustly or recognition that others are suffering. Founders' efforts usually involve serving under- or un-served individuals or redressing injurious and unfair conditions in society. Frequently these early influences are traumatic in nature. For example, an individual unjustly convicted and imprisoned because of his race founds a group to help others who are caught by discrimination in the criminal justice system. Or a woman whose child becomes ill from industrially-polluted water in her community organizes other mothers to advocate for an environmental cleanup. Coming together in a joint effort enables early supporters and founders to feel safe by connecting with like-minded peers rather than experiencing isolation and loneliness about the issue. In a basic way, the organization supports individuals harmed or traumatized to meet their own survival needs. They are held within a framework of ideas and relationships rather than excluded and left alone.

Founders need persistence, courage and strong commitment to prevail. They might have to work hard to garner attention and support from the community, or they might choose to operate out of the public eye because attention is dangerous. The organization's founders, their experiences, and their understanding of the need influence the basic definition of the organization. Both overtly through their words and phrases and arenas of attention, as well as covertly, through personality, attitude, and skills, founders establish the initial structure and process of the undertaking. These dynamics set the stage for the trauma to be embedded in the earliest aspects of the organizational culture.

Organizational creation story

The organization's early actions offer the first opportunity to define and describe itself and its place within society. These aspects form the basis of the organization's creation story. This story gives justification for the mission as well as for the style of organizational operating – what are we doing, why are we doing it, and how is it we are going about it. As an individual is empowered by being able to say who she or he is, in a similar way an organization gains self-respect and self-efficacy by this process. The first action of a rape crisis center was a "speak out" on rape. The action communicated solidarity with and support for many women who had been traumatized by sexual assault. The event went against the prevailing cultural norms of keeping silent and hiding the shame of rape. This "speak out" offered an opportunity for women to describe the trauma of rape, and those traumas were woven into the organization's creation story.

Setting and circumstances further influence the organizational creation story. Creation stories often have an element of the heroic and overcoming trauma against all odds. Organizational values, mores, and actions push against societal inequities, denial of the problem, active resistance, or hostility in the wider community. Participants in the anti-rape movement had trouble getting the wider community to take the crime of rape seriously. They advocated publicly to increase visibility and concern for rape victims. In contrast, SCS used secrecy to deal with the community's overt hostility and possible harm of gay and lesbian individuals. These experiences were incorporated into the group's creation stories, often with a lot of pride for that early courage and persistence.

Organizational moral narrative

The organization's moral narrative, its value-based explanation of its existence, adds depth to the creation story by offering a more complete framework of ideas about needs and ways to address them. That narrative is articulated at the beginning and usually changes over time as organizational members refine it. Refinements become part of the narrative, strengthening the initial articulation or shifting it in response to a changing environment or different understanding about needs. For example, SCS's moral narrative is based on its heartfelt commitment to the LGBTQ community and the acceptance and safety of the individuals who seek services. Likewise the moral narrative of anti-rape efforts was founded on a commitment to empowering women and advocating for justice, so respect for women's experiences was fundamental. Though the services in both cases changed over time, the commitment to underlying principles did not.

If part or all of an organization's moral narrative is a reaction to societal dangers and potential traumas, then the moral narrative itself includes trauma. For example, a runaway program for youth started in the early 1970s did not trust the local police to be sympathetic to runaway youth. Police represented the juvenile justice system, which meant lock up — and therefore trauma — for runaways. The staff and volunteers justified withholding information from the police in response to that perceived threat.

Values and standards inherent in the work

Crucial aspects of the work — standards and values that define its essence and the way it is to be accomplished — follow from the creation story and moral narrative. Founders' initial thinking about how to respond to needs or problems and the mission statement itself express the "right way" to approach the work. In essence, the work must be done in a particular way or with a particular approach to be true to its origins. In the examples of the rape crisis program and the runaway center, the element of individual choice for clients was crucial. This emphasis on choice respected the clients, but this approach also reinforced concerns about trauma and re-traumatization of clients and created a staff atmosphere very sensitive to power and coercion. If a candidate volunteer or staff person did not understand and agree with that approach, they would not be accepted into the organization.

Members of an organization also expect the organization to exemplify its values and standards. Especially at the beginning, homogeneous thinking helps solidify these values, and uniform behavior helps develop common ways to embody them. This consistency helps organizational members feel part of something important; they see the close connection between the harm that has occurred, the potential for more harm, the needs they are addressing, and the values-based approach they are using. These dynamics put the organization at risk for groupthink – where only agreement is allowed – and further buttress feelings of trauma and separation from the wider environment.

Boundary setting necessary for the work

Organizational boundaries define who may be served and delineate the focus of social change efforts. Boundaries help articulate who may be involved in the effort and protect those performing the organization's work. Attitude and behavior of the organization towards the wider community influence the quality of the organization's boundaries. The community may be seen as a resource to be appreciated or as a problem to be addressed. Very protective boundaries separate the organization from society and can create the feeling that there is little or no support for the organization's work. If boundaries close further, they can reinforce feelings of harassment, invisibility, fear, isolation, and menace from the wider society. These feelings add to an organizational atmosphere of vigilance and anxiety.

Identification with wider social change efforts

Finally the empathic or redemptive nature of the work itself lifts up the struggle and places it in wider social change movements. That struggle is often revealed in an organization's mission statement, which communicates an uncompromising intention about social change. The missions invite individuals to join wholeheartedly in efforts that are far-reaching and deeply important and to see themselves as defined and uplifted by their participation in those efforts. Strong identification with such high ideals and the chronic experience of falling short of meeting them is often discouraging and can be traumatizing. A colleague described this pattern as the "cycle of disappointment" that was built into the work itself.

These elements – founders' experiences, creation story, moral narrative, values and standards of the work, boundaries, and identification with the wider struggle – together create an organizational culture heavily influenced by the highly mission-driven nonprofit's work. They also provide ways that trauma can become embedded in the organization's culture. Next we explore functions of organizational culture and how those functions can lead to or reinforce trauma.

Functions of Organizational Culture

The culture of highly mission-driven nonprofits performs the following functions:

- Defines the organization's identity and uniqueness

- Provides a home for members and connects individuals to the collective identity

- Supplies language to create shared organizational knowledge and understanding

- Generates and reinforces norms that bind members to each other

- Defines the quality of relationships between the organization and the wider environment

- Enables socialization of new members

Defines the organization's identity and uniqueness

Organizational culture provides the entity with its unique positive problem-solving approach for perceived societal ills; this identity sets it apart from other organizations doing similar work. The organization's framework of understanding becomes a set of taken-for-granted assumptions that influence the ways in which organizational members perceive, think, and feel about the world. It also stabilizes the collective perception of the world and the organization's place in it. Having a rationale and acting on it creates organizational efficacy, and in turn that efficacy reinforces the organization's identity.

The organization's identity and uniqueness may revolve around trauma, for example, child abuse, the crime of rape, discrimination, and hate crimes. When the experience of trauma is central to the identity, it influences the most basic set of organizational assumptions in use. This fundamental influence sets up dynamics that eventually create a cognitive and emotional structure that is organized around trauma and traumatization. For example, early work in the field of domestic violence led to an emphasis on providing physically-safe havens for women who were abused by their husbands. Those safe havens enabled the women to leave their abusers and start another life. This approach embedded an assumption of community danger and the need for protection in these organizations' cultures.

Provides a home for members

A collective identity driven by empathic or redemptive values creates a powerful pull for individuals to take on the organization's mission as their life work. The work is perceived to be a higher calling, and individuals become part of a group that is dedicated to the organizational mission and the wider social change struggles. In return for loyalty and emotional connection to the mission, members gain a place where they can express their commitment, have their needs met, and feel uplifted about their actions. Though individuals' initial allegiance may come from their experience and passion about the issue or cause, the collective energy reinforces that allegiance and engenders fierce loyalty. One individual talked about leaving her job at a crisis agency. She said she was scared to bring up the topic with her co-workers because she feared their reactions. She knew they would consider her a traitor because she was taking a job in a different field of work. For this individual leaving her job meant being rejected by her friends and coworkers.

Individuals come to mission-driven work for a variety of professional, values-based, and personal reasons. Professional reasons include interest in nonprofit organizations, knowledge and skill development, and training. Values-based reasons include a desire to give back to the community, an aspiration to make a difference in others' lives, and a commitment to social change. Personal reasons include a sense of belonging, connection and affection; personal empowerment; and perhaps even a need for healing. Sharing these experiences and reasons provides another vehicle for trauma to be incorporated into an organization's culture.

Members also bring intense feelings and beliefs to the work, aligning their personal motivations, actions, and emotions with the mission. Alignment of individual experience and organizational mission supports an atmosphere of belonging and acceptance. Members feel valued and "at home" in expressions of passion and commitment to the work. In exchange for belonging and acceptance, members become part of a collective identity and take on the needs of the organization and those served. A Seattle Counseling Service (SCS) intern said:

> *I wanted to work with an organization that I believe in. SCS is a cornerstone of our community and truly cares about the wellbeing of all its members... Everyone who works here has an incredible knowledge base and passion for what they do. To them it is not a job but a mission to increase the overall mental health of our community (July 2010).*

All organizations, even those that do not have redemptive reasons for their existence, experience "emotional fields" (Friedman, 1985). These fields come from the normal development of emotional interdependency in a human system. Common experiences and close relationships bind individuals with emotional ties that are both intentional and unintentional. These ties play an important, albeit unacknowledged, function in the life of all organizations. Individuals' dedication to highly mission-driven nonprofits creates an especially intense atmosphere.

For many highly mission-driven groups determined attempts at social change add passion to the atmosphere. Powerful emotions inherent in empathic or redemptive work reinforce the importance and closeness of relationships. In addition these groups are partially fueled by empathy among their members. The culture, for better or worse, reflects that emotional nature and intensity. Increased intensity fuels the likelihood of trauma being embedded in the culture because the organizational structure emphasizes emotional rather than rational process. For example, meetings provide a forum for sharing emotionally-laden stories filled with individual reactions and receiving support.

Supplies language to create shared organizational knowledge

Organizational culture offers verbal, nonverbal, and symbolic language to communicate context, purpose, rationale, and values. It forms a common framework of knowledge, analysis, and practice to help members understand each other. Regular verbal and written exchanges explicitly emphasize what is important to pay attention to. Insider language reinforces members' sense of belonging and identity. Shared language also opens the door to powerful reinforcement of traumatic events and memories. Telling these trauma stories brings the particular circumstances to life and sweeps even those without the memories into the emotional field.

Equally important, the cognitive framework itself – through implicit processes – bounds the group's ideas and imagination and limits individual and collective thinking. This cognitive framework reinforces initial and current thinking about the organization's purpose and practices. Even though questions might be raised and conversations started, they stay within that thinking. Members find it hard to imagine the possibility that years of experience working on the issue did not result in a universally understood and accepted framework. This limitation manifests itself in several ways. One way is active resistance to addressing questions raised by insiders. A second is ignoring dissatisfaction from clients, community members, or funders. A third is failure to even perceive an issue or problem. A limited cognitive framework weakens an organization's ability to perceive threats and reduces its creativity in response to challenges. When this limitation occurs along with restricted boundaries, the organization begins to close in on itself.

For example, a small higher education program incorporated its values of personal exploration and self-responsibility into all aspects of its functioning. That incorporation of values became a defense mechanism against negative feedback. It was almost impossible for students to raise concerns about faculty or curriculum. Students' concerns were heard as issues of personal exploration or responsibility, rather than program-wide problems. As a result the system stayed ignorant of serious shortcomings and became used to its ignorance.

Generates and reinforces norms that bind members to each other

Organizational culture generates and reinforces norms that bind members to each other. Norms related to communication, conflict management, friendship, decision-making, power and influence, expression of feeling all serve the purpose of creating a predictable, reliable, harmonious, safe place for individuals to work. These norms develop overtly and covertly and become part of the organization's set of assumptions.

Some expectations are communicated directly and become overt norms of the group. For example, "all staff need to take turns being on call" or "oppressive language will not be tolerated." Other expectations are communicated indirectly. For example, in an organization where most staff is heterosexual, lesbian staff members find themselves quiet in conversations about family and weekend activities. Conversational cues, such as dead silence or a quick change of the subject, when they share, make them hesitant. In contrast, lesbians at SCS are more comfortable because the organizational context supports acceptance of their experiences.

When overt or covert expectations persist without being questioned, they reinforce and deepen norms without anyone's ever realizing this is happening. Similarly to how organizational language limits the conceptual reach of insiders, norms also limit what is noticed and valued, what is allowed as topics of conversation, and what is shunned and ignored. Over time norms may not remain functional for the organization. For example, the norms of secrecy and caution in SCS were essential for the early safety of its staff, volunteers and clients, but as years passed those norms got in the way of the agency's growth and development.

Norms also support the currency of conversations. When the currency is reliving work traumas, personal traumas, organizational wounding or fears related to perceived threats, the conversations center on these themes. Consequently, the norms help keep the organization focused on aspects that produce fear and anxiety. Furthermore norms are powerful influences on relationships. If norms include listening to each other and sharing concerns and stresses, then they become a vehicle for spreading traumatic stress in the organization. Norms such as these can result in a culture organized around stress and trauma.

Defines the quality of relationships with environment

An organization's culture defines the quality of relationships between the organization and the wider environment. Organizational words and symbols color the organizational perception of the community it serves. The organization might take on a heroic role in the face of out-siders' wrongdoing. Sometimes words and symbols underscore and encourage separation between organization and community. Several earlier examples of trauma depicted negative and hostile relationships between nonprofits and the wider community.

An organizational story might also emphasize differences with potential ally organizations. Organizations tell their stories in ways that make them appear distinctive and more attractive than allies doing similar work. Ironically, while this may result in funding success, this mindset creates challenges to finding like-minded collaborators. In one example, a youth-serving agency decided that it no longer needed its partner agencies to provide certain programs and so competed directly against them for funding. Its former partners referred to the agency as a "shark".

Enables socialization of new members

Organizational culture is the vehicle for socializing new members. In explicit ways certain aspects of the organization's life are shared. Prospective employees and volunteers see the mission, vision, and values on organizational websites and in information packets. New employees receive orientation and training about the visible and well-acknowledged aspects of culture; mission statements are displayed prominently on letterhead; annual reports contain a brief history of the organization and celebrate changes and advancements. Leaders and followers alike tout these aspects as emblematic of the organization's identity.

On the other hand, many cultural patterns develop in less explicit ways. These patterns are passed on to new generations of organizational members through more subtle socialization processes. New staff members learn some norms by observing how their coworkers talk, act, and respond to each other. Staff might notice a heightened emotional reaction to a situation or topic – something feels wrong – and realize that something more than the obvious is occurring. They are in the dark about exactly what is going on, but over time, they learn that certain interactions produce the same result. Staff learn to sidestep or avoid those interactions. As the socialization process continues, the organizational culture co-opts staff's thinking so they have a less-independent perspective. Eventually the power of the cultural process ensures insiders are neither aware of its subtle aspects nor the dynamics of socialization.

The organizational culture taken as a whole provides a sophisticated and persistent set of influences on all who operate within it. Those influences come from the nature of the organization's work, organizational history, and individuals who join the effort. The three aspects of work, individuals, and culture entwine with each other to create an enduring system. When the nature of the work involves trauma, organizational culture offers a powerful way for trauma and traumatization to influence all aspects of organizational life.

4

FACTORS, SUSCEPTIBILITY, AND DYNAMICS OF ORGANIZATIONAL TRAUMA

This chapter examines organizational characteristics that affect organizations' susceptibility to being traumatized and describes the dynamics of traumatized systems. It also considers how internal dynamics from earlier or ongoing trauma can be re-traumatizing to the organization. Finally it focuses on complex situations in which organizations already affected by trauma from ongoing wounding or the nature of their work are especially susceptible to single traumatizing events. The chapter ends with a vignette about an organization that suffered from various types of trauma.

Whether from single devastating events, a series of wounding actions, or the influence of the work, most highly mission-driven organizations are susceptible to traumatization. One organization may recognize and recover from a single traumatic event more quickly or more easily than another. Sometimes no one in an entity realizes damage has occurred until dysfunctional dynamics or troublesome patterns emerge. Those organizations suffer from unhealed trauma. The next section examines why some organizations are more susceptible to traumatization and less able to recover from it.

Susceptibility to Traumatization

Though we have described a variety of factors that could lead to organizational trauma, they do not inevitably lead to traumatization in all organizations experiencing them. What might account for the differences in susceptibility of organizations to becoming a traumatized system? A number of factors in an organization's life determine whether that system experiences a harmful event or ongoing pattern as organizational trauma and whether that trauma leaves a lasting influence on the organization's culture. Certain organizational strengths and characteristics cushion the impact, while some cultural patterns leave an organization more vulnerable to the trauma's deleterious effects, that is, to becoming a traumatized system.

Factors mitigating susceptibility

Organizational characteristics and strengths can mitigate effects of trauma and enhance organizational health. Presence of these features needs to be visible, widespread, universally recognized, understood, and appreciated by the organization's members in order to be effective. These features include:

- Strong core identity
- Organizational self-esteem and self-efficacy
- Facilitating structures and processes
- Hopeful and energetic leadership
- Positive connection to peer agencies

Strong core identity

An organization's core identity – its belief systems, ideals, and behavioral alignment – is expressed in its mission, vision, values, principles, and practices. This identity, which is rooted in the organizational culture, forms the bedrock of the organization's self-esteem and self-efficacy. A collective understanding of the identity, the interconnections of its elements, and how these elements are expressed in organizational life enables members to know the organization as an entity. An ongoing process of thoughtful dialogue allows the organizational culture to be a healthy living context for the organization's development. For example, the executive director of Seattle Counseling Service began a dialogue about the changing needs of the lesbian, gay, bisexual and transgendered communities and the implications of those changes for SCS's future. Without a collective dialogue, which both honored its history as a mental health agency and looked outward at the changes in the community, SCS would not have developed a wider organizational definition and broadened its mission.

Organizational self-esteem and self-efficacy

Organizational self-esteem and self-efficacy are intertwined dynamics. Self-esteem comes from a positive, secure sense of identity and enables the organization to value what it stands for. Self-efficacy enables the organization to act on its values and accomplish its goals.

The organization's history influences its self-esteem. A strong creation story with a compelling narrative of the organization's reason for existence – one that has been updated over the years – provides a framework for making sense of the organization's work and challenges. That story allows the organization to learn in an open and creative way. Organizational esteem also comes from an affirming and realistic picture of the organization. Feedback from internal and external sources allows organizational members to be informed about emerging issues and concerns. With regular feedback the organization's self-esteem is less susceptible to surprise and turbulence in its environment and within its boundaries. With this information members apply their creativity to the work and its challenges, and they renew their organization's self-image and self-esteem. With new information the organization's identity and mission stay relevant and its members stay engaged.

When the organization's self-esteem stays strong through openness and engagement, it can count on its self-efficacy to make progress, accept setbacks, learn from mistakes, and continue to move forward. The organization gains from its collective energy and avoids the pitfall of immobilization. Self-efficacy in the form of accomplishing goals and celebrating those accomplishments in turn strengthens the organization's self-esteem.

Facilitating structures and processes

Facilitating structures and processes provide universal frameworks that support the organization's operations and boundaries. Regular evaluation of staff and organizational accomplishments reinforce what has been working and what work still lies ahead. Written policies and widely known norms and expectations support an atmosphere of transparency and fairness. Discussion about mistakes engenders a sense of organizational learning and an opportunity for all to contribute. Having these structures and processes are important for several reasons. They provide balance to the emotional and passionate atmosphere of highly mission-driven nonprofits, and they interrupt the personalization of disagreements. They support looking at issues and concerns from multiple perspectives rather than a single analysis or framework. Structures and processes also enable staff to interact with each other in open and fair ways that are supported by known expectations and standards.

Hopeful and energetic leadership

Leaders strengthen their organizations by providing help, energy, and hope. They guide their organizations emotionally. Leaders act as containers for surfacing suppressed dynamics and feelings, and they model self-awareness and non-blaming dialogue. Conceptually, leaders help members see their organizations as systems and take a learning approach to organizational planning and problem solving. Leaders act in fair and transparent ways that support successful work efforts and healthy relationships. Leaders show the way through acting with their own enthusiasm, optimism, and confidence about the future. They also provide ways to talk about hope, energy, and spirit, and they nurture organizational members' optimism for positive change.

Positive connection to peer agencies

Connections to peer agencies, external groups that mirror the organization's aspirations and hopes, provide inspiration and new ideas as well as sources of help in difficult times. In earlier examples agency executive directors Maureen and Linda counted on help from leaders in peer agencies when they were facing tough situations. Similarly to the positive benefits of individuals banding together for a purpose, organizations that can band together through cooperative actions, honest dialogue, and a unified approach on potentially divisive issues stand a better chance of weathering difficult times. More importantly, these connections provide the organization an ongoing opportunity to learn about itself and its place in the larger environment.

Factors exacerbating susceptibility

We have seen several patterns that weaken an organization and increase its susceptibility to traumatization. When these patterns occur, an organization's culture is not as robust as it could be, and in some stressed circumstances these patterns compromise the organization's ability to make sense of its experiences and relate effectively to its environment. These patterns include:

- Limiting attitudes and worldview set at the organization's creation

- Unproductive relationships between organization and environment

- Organizational amnesia

- Unrecognized wounding from previous traumas

Limiting attitudes and worldview

Founders' and early leaders' experiences of trauma influence the original reasons and assumptions for the organization's existence. Leaders collectively set an attitude for organizational discourse based on their motivations and build rationales for their attitudes. For example, members of a church found a runaway girl overdosed on drugs in their parking lot. The members were deeply disturbed by this tragedy. They discovered that society often treated vulnerable runaway youth very poorly, jailing them. The church members were appalled by this and decided to take action by creating a safe haven for runaways. Early volunteers said:

> We decided that we would be successful if we helped one young person get a better handle on their life.
>
> We were susceptible to hearing the young people's stories and being on their side. We had a direct line to their trauma and it affected our organization's way of being.

This group was predisposed to suffer from cumulative trauma because of their depth of commitment to these abused and exploited youth.

Other historical factors may also play a part in an organization's susceptibility to traumatization. The wider community may deny or minimize the problem – through inadvertent or willful ignorance or overt hostility towards the entity trying to provide services or change societal attitudes about the issue. The organization's response is distrust and a protective distance from its wider environment. The protective distance becomes part of the organization's core identity, leaving it susceptible to patterns of distrust, outrage, and helplessness.

For example, a runaway youth agency was trying to change societal attitudes about youth who ran away from home. The general public opinion was that runaway centers encouraged young people to run away. The centers set up to protect youth were being blamed for the problem. When staff offered educational events about reasons youth might leave home, they were met with skepticism. These early community encounters left the organization feeling isolated and unsupported.

In many situations earliest attitudes, formed at a vulnerable time in the organization's development, continued to influence its life. The organization exists within an environment but does not see the community as a resource. Protectiveness cuts off the organization from signals in the external environment about the need to change. These dynamics create gaps in useful information and learning as well as loss of collegiality, support, and inspiration. In extreme cases wariness and protectiveness define the organization's culture. When traumas occur, such isolated organizations have few coping resources and are more susceptible to traumatization.

Unproductive relationships

Ongoing harassment, threats, and attitudes of indifference or hostility from the community underscore an organization's separation. The organization anticipates battles and struggles and creates organizational defenses predicated on an unsympathetic or antagonistic community. These organizational responses buttress attitudes that leave the entity cut off from its community and allies. The organization loses information, perspective, and energy. For example, a rape crisis agency began a precipitous decline after its last permanent executive director left. When board and staff realized the seriousness of their situation, they did not know where to turn for help. They had isolated themselves from other agencies and did not trust outsiders or understand what resources were available.

Organizational amnesia

Sometimes organizations suffer from "organizational amnesia", a forgetting of early history and founding principles and values. These organizations address current challenges and opportunities as if they were brand new. Members have no awareness of how often these dynamics have occurred during the organization's history. They do not understand the impact of these dynamics on their organization's development. When separated from its own history in this way, the organization as a whole may miss the significance of certain events. An event might seem insignificant in the moment, but relate directly back to previous negative occurrences in the organization's history. Without recognizing the connections to organizational history staff and board members play out value or structural conflicts in interpersonal arenas. The situation and relationships worsen because no one sees the larger pattern. When this happens, the organization cannot learn from its experience. These gaps in learning leave dynamics unaddressed or purposely buried and create a subsequent amnesia about organizational history.

For example, an executive director left his position after a short tenure. Fear pervaded the organization, productivity declined, and some staff resigned. The organization went into a tailspin as board members tried to understand what had happened and why. No insiders remembered or acknowledged that similar events and consequences had occurred twice in the past seven years. During those previous periods the organization was unsettled, and staff members coped on their own. The organization as a whole never looked at the circumstances under which leaders seemed to leave. Eventually the agency gained clarity about leader turnover patterns but only after a painful period of turmoil.

Unrecognized trauma

Some organizations are more susceptible to traumatization because they suffer from the deleterious effects of unacknowledged previous traumas. Organizational leaders and members notice and complain about negative behaviors of individuals, but they do not recognize the signs and symptoms of organizational distress. Supervisors focus on helping individuals cope better with the effects of the work by offering self-care strategies and coaching. Even trainings about vicarious trau-matization remain focused on individuals and their capacity to cope. Ultimately managers encourage troubled staff to leave. In focusing on individuals everyone misses organizational patterns, such as low wages, unrealistic expectations, problematic boundaries, and pervasive fear, all of which might be fueling individual distress and collective trauma.

For example, an advocacy program operated within a larger non-profit. Joe, a program manager, was unable to make headway in turn-ing around the negative team atmosphere. It seemed to him that the members of the team just did not get along well with each other. He sought help from an outside consultant. The team was described as feeling helpless and anxious, and team members communicated a collective heaviness and little hope for change. They lacked coopera-tive energy and seemed to feel that the program had been abandoned by the parent organization. It turned out that there had been a very poorly managed transition with the previous program director and a long gap of leadership for the group. This experience was described as traumatic for the team who received no help from the larger sys-tem in addressing the harmful impacts. In fact the team thought that the parent organization did not even recognize the team's pain. Once this history was acknowledged and the impact addressed by team leaders, the team as a whole had more energy to improve its internal dynamics and move forward.

Any organization that suffers a single devastating traumatic event may be left reeling. However, when an organization has already been weak-ened by the dynamics of unacknowledged trauma or ongoing wound-ing, it can be permanently damaged from that single event because it has so few coping resources.

Whatever its history, if an organization has sufficient strengths and resources to mitigate its susceptibility to traumatization, it may recover relatively quickly from a traumatic event. If an organization does not have sufficient resources, including an understanding of what it is experiencing, it will likely end up a traumatized system. The following section describes what a traumatized system looks like.

Organizational Traumatization Syndrome

The syndrome of a traumatized system is comprised of multiple dynamics present in the organization. The existence of one dynamic does not mean the system is traumatized, but in a traumatized system a preponderance of these dynamics will be evident. We describe those dynamics separately but recognize that they mutually influence each other and together constitute the syndrome. These dynamics are:

- Closed boundaries between organization and external environment

- Centrality of insider relationships

- Stress and anxiety contagion

- Inadequate worldview and identity erosion

- Depression expressed through fear or anger

- Despair and loss of hope

Closed boundaries between organization and external environment

To the extent that an organization experiences or perceives its environment to be unsupportive and hostile, it protects itself. The external environment (they) is vilified while the organization (we) is idealized. Boundaries become less permeable and less information and energy enters. The organization does not take in information from the external environment and does not accept or make use of feedback. Ultimately the organizational system closes down and allows little outside information to penetrate. With little new information the system tends towards group thinking, sameness, self-justification, and resistance to change.

As the system's boundaries close and information is constricted, the organization becomes incapable of correctly assessing external reality. Its self-image becomes distorted. Constriction and distortion create a dangerous situation for the organization. Possibly at the height of its need for outside support and help, the organization is least able to ask for and receive it.

Leaders whom we interviewed described how long it took them to see that something was terribly wrong inside their organizations. In some circumstances the leaders were shocked and bewildered from a single tragic event and focused on their own coping. In other cases they missed patterns because they were completely caught up in dysfunctional dynamics. In some cases they were predisposed to distrusting outsiders and "going it alone" rather than asking for help. In many cases they had no ideas about what help was available or how to access that help.

Centrality of insider relationships

Closed boundaries shut out the external environment and intensify internal organizational life; insider relationships take on greater importance. For various reasons the organization's culture can already have an intense emotional atmosphere. Traumatic occurrences deepen that intensity. When in a traumatized system, insiders have nowhere else to turn except to each other. With a feeling of "us against the world", members turn inward for safety, support and comfort. They emphasize loyalty and caring for each other and show it by empathic listening to each other's concerns and stresses. They also demonstrate it by reinforcing heroic efforts that emphasize the importance of their work. To ensure that this safe and comforting atmosphere continues less difference of opinion is tolerated. Staff avoid conflict with each other. Even so, many staff members report vacillating between honesty and loyalty. A former staff member of a youth-serving agency remarked that he felt in solidarity with his peers about the mission but not a lot of trust in his co-workers. For this person relationships became more intense and more intimate but paradoxically less safe.

Stress and anxiety contagion

Outsiders are not trusted, the boundaries have tightened, and those inside the organization have nowhere to turn but to each other. The stress of the system is kept within. Predisposed to think about the struggles and challenges of their work in similar ways because of the cultural patterns in place, members become swept up in co-workers' feelings, anxieties, and stresses. This dynamic overloads the stress-absorption capacity of the organization. The internal atmosphere remains stressful, and stress becomes a central lens through which the work is experienced. This results in a culture partially defined by its stress. A former staff at a domestic violence agency told the story of her first days there:

> I was brand new and getting an orientation to the agency. As I listened to my co-workers talk about their work with clients, I found myself tensing up. I realized that they were describing their work in terms of its stress and toll. There I was feeling as stressed as they were without having had any contact with clients.

This new staff person caught the stress of her colleagues, and it became part of her emotional response to being at work.

Inadequate worldview and identity erosion

When its organizing principles and practices can no longer account for the experiences of its members and its relationships, the organization's identity begins to unravel. The values and principles of the work are undermined, lost over time, or egregiously breached. Severe harm to the organization's values and self-worth might come to light suddenly.

For example, a program within a public school district was dedicated to creating opportunities for minority-owned businesses to compete successfully for contracts with the school district. A state audit uncovered numerous examples of questionable, possibly illegal, actions, and stories of staff who were told to keep quiet by managers when they raised concerns. This program's identity was shaken to its core; its laudable purpose was completely destroyed, and it quickly fell into disrepute and disarray. Behaviors of powerful staff betrayed the program's purpose and eroded its identity. The program was dismantled, and key leaders in the district administration lost their positions.

Identity erosion could also arise from dysfunctional organizational patterns. Even under normal circumstances, anxiety in human systems undermines norms of openness and creativity and lessens safety and trust. In traumatized systems organizational life constricts. In heightened stress and anxiety-filled circumstances, insiders seek to make sense of their experiences while avoiding the reality that trust has eroded. They sidestep or suppress any conflict that could divide them. Their interactions end up reinforcing common thoughts, beliefs, and fears. Only the most easily-agreed-upon understandings of what is happening hold up. It is safer to blame outsiders for the disturbing feelings, so members focus on hostility, lack of justice, or other negative perceptions about the external environment. Surface harmony holds because dissenting voices fall silent and disagreements are repressed.

Emotional constriction leads to cognitive constriction of the organization's worldview. This constricted organizational worldview distorts the way most external and internal events are experienced and interpreted. In very polarized situations, meaning making revolves around a perception that everything outside the organization is corrupt, immoral, and untrustworthy while everything inside the organization is good, moral, and right. This shrunken worldview along with closed boundaries compromises the organization's ability to respond to external information and pressures and to plan for its own future.

Depression expressed through fear or anger

Insularity, widespread stress, and a constricted worldview based on fear and anxiety lead to the dynamic of organizational depression. Closed boundaries reduce exchange of information and energy with the external environment. Without access to external perspective and energy the system loses vitality and perspective. Unabated fear and anxiety worsen. Recurring conversations among staff are aimed at supporting and bolstering each other. However, because members are constricted by their common worldview and language, these conversations do not succeed in their purpose. In telling each other the same stories over and over again the same feelings of helplessness and anger are triggered. These stories act like organizational flashback mechanisms. With no way to break this cycle of re-triggering or re-traumatizing, the staff members become less able to carry out organizational tasks. Productivity in accomplishing the work of the mission is subsumed by endless processing conversations that serve to further reinforce the dynamics just described.

Individuals in one agency reported being overwhelmed, demoralized, angered, and ashamed. They felt a loss of civility and increase in hostility. Staff stayed away from staff meetings so as to not experience the negative atmosphere.

> *The combination of all those things was so awful and so overwhelming.*

> *We were stuck in a downward spiral.*

> *We were in a trance state. Like hypnotized robots – not recognizing our choices*

Despair and loss of hope

Depleted by a lack of organizational efficacy and feelings of victimization and holding on to a view of the world as uncaring and unchanging, the organization begins to despair. The organization's boundaries have closed down, organizational members have focused inward, and depression has set in. The organizational culture, already fueled by passion for its mission, becomes hypersensitive to the internal existence of what it wants to change in the world. This hypersensitivity is exacerbated by the organization's isolation from the wider society. As it cannot succeed in changing its external environment, it also cannot succeed in changing itself. Ultimately, the organization loses the ability to make meaning of its work and to connect to wider purposes and movements. Its spirit and energy are exhausted. In the worst situations the organization is left with insufficient energy to keep going. Staff and board members leave in waves, or the organization collapses inward and gives up on itself. In one agency the board members used phrases like "We had no emotional energy left" and "It's like we were infected by a terrible cancer" to describe their experience. The work comes to a standstill until finally the agency closes its doors.

Though we have described these dynamics separately, pragmatically speaking they are interconnected and mutually reinforcing. Closed boundaries offer little new energy or perspective to organizational processes. Continuing to view the world as uncaring and unchanging reinforces protective boundaries. Both promote over-involvement in internal processes and distract the organization from its mission. This distraction in turn exacerbates the feelings of hopelessness about making any real impact on the wider society. Depression, despair, and loss of hope are both cause and result of the other dynamics.

All of these dynamics – closed boundaries, centrality of insider relationships, stress and anxiety contagion, inadequate or constricted worldview, depression, and despair and loss of hope – operate in open and hidden ways and result in a cumulative impact on the organization. Because they may not be recognized and named easily, they also have a re-traumatizing effect. The longer these dynamics persist unnoticed and unaddressed the further they weaken the organization.

The following story about the Welfare Rights Organizing Coalition (WROC), an organization that experienced various kinds of trauma and traumatization, helps to illuminate many aspects of this chapter.

WROC's Story

WROC started in the mid-1980s and closed its doors suddenly in spring of 2007. Its mission was to work toward social justice by empowering low-income families, especially those on welfare, to effect positive change in their lives and communities. Much of its success was due to the tremendous energy and commitment of its executive director, Jean Colman, who served in a leadership role for nearly twenty years. Pat met Jean just after she started working at WROC, and then Pat worked on various initiatives with the organization until the mid-2000s. With Pat's help WROC completed an intensive organizational assessment and a three-year strategic plan.

We pick up the story in 2004. Jean and Pat were talking about how to proceed with intended strategic changes at WROC. Jean knew that her talents were better used in organizing efforts and that someone else could do administrative tasks more efficiently. Jean wanted WROC to expand its membership statewide, and this role switch would make it possible. When Pat and Jean started talking about specific ways to proceed, Jean hesitated. She talked about the dire realities of the organization:

> *I have to raise money to meet payroll next month, our grants are less secure now than they were last year, and no one wants to assume the board presidency. Board members have so much going on in their lives that they cannot pay attention to WROC. There is no one else but me to be responsible for all of this.*

Whew! It seemed to Pat that whenever she and Jean met they had the same conversation. WROC was not achieving financial or structural stability, let alone embarking on the expansion Jean envisioned. Pat began to see the parallels between families on welfare and WROC. Like its members who depended on public assistance, WROC was just keeping its head above water. She wondered if WROC was actually suffering from unacknowledged organizational trauma, and if understanding that might help the organization in some way.

WROC seemed like a classic redemptive organization, and several patterns stood out to Pat. The first related to the societal perception of women on welfare, who were judged negatively and shown little empathy by the wider community. WROC's creation story captured this experience of a largely uncaring and hostile society and a determination to help lower-income women achieve fair treatment and dignity. Organizational values included strong and vigilant action, which was believed necessary to address threats to single mothers. WROC members could not and would not give up. Keeping up the fight, despite defeats and exhaustion, was the WROC way. Pat thought this pattern led to collective staff and volunteer fatigue and a chronic feeling of organizational depletion.

The second pattern related to the parallel between the realities of low-income parents and WROC. The parents, who were the mainstay of the membership, struggled on a daily basis to make ends meet. They saw welfare grants go down while their living expenses went up. For the members and the organization itself, there seemed to be a chronic scarcity and fear of losing what they had. Individual and organizational advocacy centered on protecting what little they had. This pattern reinforced the necessity for protection and a sense of scarcity.

In addition, WROC organized its advocacy around confrontation – with local welfare offices, with funders, with legislators, with public officials, and with community members. This approach seemed to result in an ongoing sense of battle. WROC experienced many failures in its attempts to gain support on its issues. Individual WROC members and staff coped with that sense of battle and failure on their own. Their way of thinking was, "What did you expect? Just move on to the next task." This attitude made it difficult to acknowledge openly the ongoing toll of the work on individuals. Feelings of stress played out as undercurrents. In many cases individuals dropped out of sight and communication.

When Pat shared some of her thinking, Jean recognized the influences on the organization. The existing dynamics from Jean's perspective were "the reality of our advocacy work. We are always getting in someone's face about what is wrong with the system." Despite the conversation, it seemed to Pat that Jean never saw the patterns as being directly connected to WROC's redemptive work of changing societal attitudes towards public assistance. While Jean saw the influences at some level, she did not see the organization's accumulating trauma.

The situation worsened significantly in 2006. Unhappy members held secret meetings, and negative and hurtful public communications signaled to the community that something was wrong. Jean realized that WROC was in trouble but did not ask for any outside help. She decided against holding any organizational meetings with staff and parent members. She thought that the situation included a number of problems that she could address separately. Though concerned, Jean believed that working on important tasks would take care of the dissension. She was "moving on to the next task."

Dissension continued. In the winter of 2007 individuals who were unhappy with WROC joined the board of directors. Shortly afterwards the board fired Jean and laid off the only other staff person. When WROC members and outside funding entities questioned the board members about their actions, board members stayed silent. The board isolated itself from everyone and continued operating in secrecy for a few more months. They closed WROC's door that spring.

In a reflective conversation with students a year later Jean saw the trouble as her fault as WROC's leader. She felt that if she could have gotten discussion going on the important organizational tasks, the situation would have improved. Jean did not make the connection between the toll the work was taking on her and the organization and WROC's inability to solve its problems or accomplish tasks.

Pat thought WROC had reached a point where its internal reserves were depleted. Suddenly laying off its long-time leader and second paid staff traumatized the depleted organization. Its boundaries closed, and dissension within the organization during the last months made it impossible to focus on WROC's future. Depression and despair set in. The organization needed an infusion of fresh energy and broader perspective, but it could not reach out to its supporters and allies. With no energy it had no future.

What might have made a difference in this situation? Knowledge about the cumulative trauma and redemptive work might have helped WROC members, including the board, see the situation more broadly and find ways to strengthen the organization itself. Understanding the realities of redemptive organizations could open dialogue among members and staff about how to deal with the toll of the work. Open conversations about collective exhaustion might have helped support those who otherwise dropped out. If WROC's boundaries had remained open, more people who cared might have become involved. Individuals could have helped contain conflict and stop the downward spiral. Infusion of new energy and optimism would have lifted the organization's spirits and helped determine a way forward.

Conclusion

Chapters One, Two, Three, and Four form the foundation of the concepts related to organizational trauma: the definition of organizational trauma and its place among other dynamics related to organizational life, the understanding of how the nature of an organization's work influences the culture of that organization, and specific factors related to the occurrence of trauma and it dynamics. The next chapter is based on an extensive study of a rape crisis center that closed in the late 1990s after almost thirty years of serving the community. It is a cautionary tale that shows how many facets of the four earlier chapters played out in one organization's life.

5

DEATH OF A RAPE CRISIS CENTER

In this chapter we share the story of a rape crisis center that closed after almost thirty years serving victims of sexual assault. It was one of the first sexual assault crisis centers in the nation and the first one on the west coast. A small group of volunteers from a YWCA organized it in 1972. When the agency closed, it was part of a network of accredited sexual assault programs with four peer agencies serving sexual assault survivors in the same county. This agency provided services by a large cadre of volunteers, and advocacy and community education by a group of staff members. It stood out among its peers in its dedication to serving marginalized communities, such as lesbian, gay, transgendered, and bisexual individuals, homeless youth, women in the sex industry, and people of color.

Its closure in 1999 surprised and puzzled us. As we developed and refined our ideas about organizational trauma, we returned to what happened at this rape crisis center. We conducted extensive research into the agency's culture and closure and searched for incidents and patterns of traumatization (Hormann and Vivian, 2004). We concluded there was a set of interrelated factors that led to its eventual closure:

- Organizational culture, which showed characteristics consistent with the impact of cumulative trauma from its empathic and redemptive work

- Two traumatizing events, eight years apart, related to leaders leaving

- A cascading series of wounding events that re-traumatized the agency after the last permanent executive director departed.

Organizational Culture

In thinking about its culture, we identified three interlocking pairs of organizational characteristics (See Table 5.1). Each pair created dysfunctional patterns over time. These dysfunctional patterns in turn created a culture susceptible to destabilization by traumatic occurrences and compromised the agency's ability to address these traumas and heal itself.

Mission-driven and feminist is the first pair of organizational characteristics. From its beginning the rape crisis center radiated passion and commitment and an excitement about women helping women. Its efforts rested on a philosophy of choice and empowerment for victims/survivors. These qualities were owned and perceived as strengths. Over time they led to another set of characteristics among staff and volunteers including: emphasis on self-empowerment, an expectation of interpersonal caring and support, and an intense emotional atmosphere.

The importance of relationships and ambivalence about power and leadership make up the second pair. Consistent with its feminist roots, the agency relied on relation-based structures and processes to create an inclusive, egalitarian and nonhierarchical organization. Volunteers, staff, and board members formed, maintained, and protected friendships. Participatory decision-making was used. Over time these characteristics led to confusion about power and authority, distrust of leaders, and unconstructive ways of dealing with conflict.

Table 5.1. Paired Characteristics

Paired Cultural Aspects	Organizational Strengths	Organizational Shadows
Mission driven and Feminist	Passion, commitment and excitement about helping women Philosophy of choice Empowerment for victims/survivors	Over-emphasis on self-empowerment Expectation of interpersonal caring and support Intense emotional atmosphere
Importance of relationships and Ambivalence about power and leadership	Relationship-oriented Importance of friendships Inclusive, egalitarian and nonhierarchical Participatory decision-making	Confusion about power and authority Distrust of leaders Unconstructive ways of dealing with conflict
Institutional racism and Commitment to anti-oppression philosophy and work	Awareness of inequities Commitment to diversity Concern about racism	Emotional intensity Critique and self-consciousness Hurt and suspicion Abiding tension around issues of race and oppression

Institutional (organizational and movement) racism and commitment to anti-oppression philosophy and work form the third pair of characteristics. Almost from the beginning, women of color noticed and objected to the white feminist philosophy being articulated and the lack of sensitivity to issues raised by women of color. At the same time white women, though naive in retrospect, voiced passionate commitment to diversity and concern about racism. Misperception and misunderstanding became features of conversations addressing racism. Over time this set of characteristics led to other patterns: emotional intensity, critique and self-consciousness, hurt and suspicion, and an abiding tension around issues of race and oppression.

Mission-driven

This agency's mission was compelling and pervasive. Interviewees from the 1970s described the immediate purposes as helping to reduce the physical and emotional trauma caused by rape and to mitigate the humiliation women suffered from medical, police, and court procedures. The agency also had the larger purposes of changing society's attitudes about rape and working to prevent rape from occurring. By the mid-1990s the description of the mission read:

> We are a nonprofit, community based organization
> confronting the issue of sexual violence. We work to
> empower survivors and their significant others through
> counseling and advocacy services. We strive to reduce sexual
> violence through education. We are committed to provide
> services that are culturally appropriate and accessible.
> Recognizing the connections between sexual violence and
> all forms of oppression, we are dedicated to social change.

These mission statements were grand, compelling, and important. Founders commented:

> Women were dealing with issues that were their
> issues. It was amazing how much work got done with

volunteers...It was a pretty heady time regarding common commitment.

There was a sense of the ability to make major changes that has stayed with me to this day.

In the 1980s individuals spoke about their commitment to providing services and to changing the world. Some examples:

It was a privilege to work with survivors on their journeys and with folks who shared your passion and dream of a future without violence.

We were a talented group of women and men, staff and volunteers, who believed in what we were doing and that we could make a change in the world.

In the 1990s commitment to the mission of providing services and changing the world continued. However, the increasing emphasis on anti-oppression is evident:

I trained the volunteer advocate/counselors. It was a combination of indoctrination and evangelical function... Half the training hours were anti-oppression training so people learned to be part of the agency culture.

There was a huge emphasis on cultural diversity. Cultural competence was included in everything we did. We were one of the first rape relief organizations to have outreach, and we were aware that you couldn't just send anybody — you needed a person who represented the community.

Feminist

The agency's feminist foundation came from two sources: Giving voice to women's issues and developing nonhierarchical ways to organize the agency. Those involved in the 1970s commented:

The YWCA was the hotbed of activist feminism. We had a history of pushing the edges of dealing with women's issues in an aggressive, supportive-of-women way.

We worked with victims of sexual assault. We were committed to providing the services to victims ... they were encouraged to make their own decisions about their care, about whether to go to the police.

Many spoke about the commitment to a nonhierarchical structure and egalitarian leadership:

Hierarchy was being questioned philosophically, and organizations... we were exploring alternative ways to organize the work.

It was a grassroots organization, participatory at all levels—board, staff, and volunteers.

At its heyday, [it was a] culture of truth and honesty and women feeling their power... So people battled all the time—and conflict was handled in a way that was progressive and experimental.

Importance of relationships

Relationships were central to this organization's culture. Women across the decades spoke about bonding with like-minded women and making lifelong friendships.

There was social overlap with work stuff. It was very fun and felt like family at times. We all went out dancing.

Staff were diverse, smart, interesting, fun women...I liked hanging out with staff; there was a social element based on shared politics.

r...People were good
ending on what was

ration between personal needs
ational needs...I observed that
intertwined in one another.

the late 1990s depict a greater intensity to

*sphere was intense. We got our social needs met
there. No one dated, no outside activities, no vacation.*

*There was always intense emotion on the staff. We
would have a staff meeting every Tuesday — very intense
with someone always crying. Then we had a two-hour
lunch and spent the afternoon making each other laugh.*

Ambivalence about power and leadership

Interviewees in all decades described ambivalence about power and leadership. That ambivalence seemed to play out in ambiguous structures and resistance to hierarchy. Individuals from the 1970s commented:

*We were unclear about how democratic/egalitarian the
decision-making process was.*

*The tension, confusion, and ambivalence about
decision-making were a pervasive problem.*

The ambivalence persisted into the 1980s:

*It was a participatory organization; it was not supposed
to be hierarchical. I think that was a problem area. We
wanted everyone to be involved in every decision.*

> *There was an evolution...from a grassroots bunch of
> women to an external accountability/structure...That
> was at odds with our internal culture, which was still a
> throwback to the feminist revolutionary days.*

The 1990s saw no change in these dynamics. Comments from board members and staff included:

> *Lack of structure, lack of empowerment for staff, lack of
> leadership (chaos), and no authority*

> *Nonhierarchical decision making requires trust and does
> not work when there isn't any...The director has inherent
> power. Any action on her part equals misuse of power.*

> *Staff were an amazing bunch and then they got
> dragged down into the power and oppression dynamics
> and got stuck in them...They thought that the agency
> was theirs.*

> *It was a problem that employees had a say in
> everything. The staff were running the store...No one
> on the board was willing to take over the organization.*

Ambivalence about power and leadership seemed to intensify during leadership transitions. A few went smoothly, but many were interpersonally difficult and organizationally disruptive. One leader from the 1970s recounted being "voted out" of the agency after she had resigned. "It was a bitter ending. I was made to feel like a non-person." Another leader from that decade, having resigned from her position, was asked to leave the organization altogether because she was "too powerful."

Even an executive director from the early 1980s who left voluntarily commented that, "We got through the blowout of people being furious with me, and at that point, I knew it was time to go." A new executive director was hired, and not long into that executive director's tenure, tension about power and leadership surfaced. "Staff did not understand how nonprofits ran. They thought I had too much power." In 1987 this executive director left amidst accusations of abuse of power and racism. Her sudden departure is one of the traumatic events discussed later in this chapter.

Many individuals involved in the agency during the early 1990s commented on the difficulty of making the co-director model work. "We implemented a different structure [co-directors] and still had some of the same problems." In the mid-1990s one co-director, a woman of color, was fired and again the agency spent a year exploring alternative governance structures. This is the second traumatic event described later in this chapter.

Rather than talk directly with each other about the tensions related to power, racism, and leadership, the staff and board focused on the structure of management. This exploration and redesign of management seemed to be one way that this agency as an organization played out its ambivalence about power and leadership.

Institutional racism

Throughout this crisis center's history the issues of agency racism and agency commitment to social change and anti-oppression efforts were inextricably tied together. Racism existed through lack of cultural sensitivity (a phrase not even used during its early history) and a philosophy and structure dominated by the white-feminist movement. At the same time a sincere commitment to change the world and eliminate oppression inspired many staff and volunteers. These two realities chafed and then rubbed raw internal relationships and relationships between the agency and its peers in the anti-rape movement.

Issues related to race were first raised in the 1970s and became more pronounced as time passed. Concerns mirrored those voiced about the women's movement as a whole. Both women of color and white women voiced them:

I remember bemoaning the fact that we were all white.

There was a struggle for women of color with white women who didn't want to share power...Some of the worst racism came from the upper echelons.

There was not a way to deal with the subtle racism.

During the 1970s and early to mid-1980s the agency did not directly address issues of power and racism within the organization. It focused on actions; it developed outreach programs to communities of color and other underserved populations and began hiring a more diverse staff. As the staff and communities served became more diverse, the need to confront issues of racism also intensified. Said staff from the 1980s:

There was a diversity of religion, class, ethnicity, race, and sexual preference...None of us had lived and worked in this type of organization before coming here.

There was a lot of covert racism.

Staff of color in the 1990s voiced similar concerns:

The women of color were 'problematized'.

The women of color on staff had conflict with the board. They wrote a letter, wanting an apology and the resignation of some board members. I signed that letter. I needed to go, because of my position, and by getting rid of me, it kept the women of color under control. It was a powerful message.

The agency, despite its anti-oppression values, never found ways to communicate effectively across multiple differences and address issues of internal racism satisfactorily. Rather it developed a pattern of focusing on surface behaviors and problems and avoiding collective discussions about racism and its impact on the organizational culture.

Commitment to anti-oppression philosophy and work

In the 1970s staff and volunteers spoke of stopping rape, changing the world, making the world a safe place for women. Members experienced each change in law, change in law enforcement procedure, and change in institutional response to rape victims as a social change victory. In the 1980s, influenced by the broader social change movements and its own internal tension around racism, the agency focused its social change thinking on working to increase its outreach to diverse communities. A conscious decision during this era to significantly increase the diversity of staff and volunteers also reflected social change thinking.

By the 1990s, the agency's direct services and social change efforts were strongly—almost solely—grounded in anti-oppression philosophy.

An outside supporter commented:

> They saw, talked, and worked sexual assault as part of oppression – in contrast to other programs that were helping victims of sexual assault.

A staff said:

> There was a core training program that included anti-oppression training...I learned a lot about sexual violence and the path to oppression.

In an attempt to address institutional racism, the co-director model of the 1990s mandated that at least one co-director be a woman of color. Concerns about racism and ambivalence about power and leadership blended together in the governance structure. Several individuals who were involved during that period mentioned a renewed agency emphasis on anti-oppression work and internal tension and self-consciousness about how to behave in a nonracist and non-oppressive manner:

> People did not want to be labeled racist or homophobic so things were not addressed until they were staring

> *you in the face, e.g., someone was about to be fired...*
> *We wanted to be politically correct.*

As the mission and work became more centrally influenced by an anti-oppression analysis, that framework was used to explain dynamics within the agency. As they deepened their understanding of oppression, staff became more sensitized to those dynamics inside the agency and the movement. The sophistication of its analysis kept the agency in an almost continual turmoil. Women of color and white women, individuals inside and outside the agency, described that intensity:

> *I felt unsafe. My credibility as a white middle class,*
> *well-educated woman was always being challenged.*

> *The agency's anti-oppression philosophy was intense.*
> *You had to 'get it' to be a staff or volunteer and could*
> *not waver or doubt. Scrutiny later became brutal.*

> *One staff believed in this world that we had created,*
> *that racism wouldn't play a part. Ultimately it was*
> *so hurtful because the structure responded in a racist*
> *way...No matter what the ideology of the system, it is*
> *dangerous to forget you are a woman of color.*

From a state coalition member:

> *We experienced them as cranky. Nothing we did was*
> *right or good enough. They were the holders of anti-*
> *oppression work and the only ones who did it right.*

This rape crisis center was seen to be "old school" in its organizational culture – commitment to a collective and feminist approach to governance, emphasis on utilizing volunteers to deliver services when other agencies moved to paid professional staff, and an edgy uncompromising approach to social change and anti-oppression work. Its culture set the organization apart from its peer agencies.

Their strength was their challenging. They were more unified in their agency mission than unified with the system of which they were a part. They were fierce in their critique.

This separation, coupled with the agency's intense internal dynamics and central focus on interpersonal relationships, played a significant part in the events of its last year. The separation kept the community members in the dark about what was occurring and reduced the agency's avenues of support. In turn, community ignorance and lack of support encouraged further isolation of the agency. These organizational patterns increased the agency's susceptibility to traumatization over the years, and in its last year reinforced the dynamics of a traumatized system – closed boundaries, centrality of insider relationships, stress and anxiety contagion, depression, and an inadequate worldview. Eventually, in its last months of existence, the organization lost hope.

Cumulative Trauma from Empathic and Redemptive Work

The agency suffered from cumulative traumatization because of the nature of its work. Its work demanded deep commitment and carried risks of failure, rejection, and marginalization. Staff and volunteers across the decades commented about how hard it was to listen to the stories and hear about another's pain and trauma:

The constant exposure to stories of trauma was hard.

We need to be there for others. Our self-care strategies were too superficial.

To work on the line was really hard. It made me exasperated and sad. It made me see most men as potential rapists for a while.

I needed a lot of support during that time because it was just so heart-wrenching.

Others commented about the difficulty of social change work:

> *Most people got burned out working with victims. We were only able to be 'Band-Aids' instead of solving the larger problem.*

Over time the organization viewed the external environment as ignorant, uncaring, and sometimes hostile, and it developed a self-righteous attitude in response.

> *I participated in a lot of anti-oppression training...I had a lot of pain and anger about racism...I felt anger and hatred at men. Men are bad and women are good.*

The rape crisis center's intense social change stance increased its isolation from other organizations in the movement and the community at large. This isolation in turn reinforced the importance of internal relationships, processes, and dynamics. Closed agency boundaries blocked new perspectives and energy and kept the emotional intensity trapped inside. That internal preoccupation acted as a defense mechanism against the guilt and anxiety associated with making little headway in its anti-oppression work to end sexual assault. This isolation and preoccupation undermined the agency's ability to see outsiders as resources and ask for help. Said a staff from the 1990s:

> *Our group was always so insular. We rarely asked for help from people outside the agency and when we did, if we didn't agree, we often dismissed it. That dynamic made [any] internal crisis so much worse because there was nowhere to turn except to each other, and there was no perspective, no bigger picture.*

Cumulative trauma from the nature of its work embedded itself in this organization's culture and it took its toll on staff, board members, and volunteers. The agency's health and sustainability were also compromised by two specific traumatic events.

Unhealed Traumatic Events

Our research about leadership transitions in the mid-1980s and mid-1990s led us to believe that both instances were unhealed traumatic events for the agency. Individuals involved in the events did not necessarily name them as traumatic, though they did use language consistent with traumatic events and traumatized systems to describe their experiences. In both occurrences individuals and groups within the agency attempted to address the seriousness of the situations, but they missed the core wounding and exacerbating organizational patterns at work. The aftereffects of both events were embedded in the agency's culture; their impact intensified dysfunctional patterns and weakened the agency.

In the mid-1980s the executive director of six years suddenly left. In the mid-1990s one co-director, a woman of color, was fired. Both events were surprises to practically all involved and remained undiscussed and mysterious. Both events destabilized the agency for a period of time and consumed large amounts of organizational energy. They left unhealthy and unaddressed dynamics that surfaced in indirect ways in subsequent years. Those dynamics connected directly to organizational unease about power and leadership and to tension around racism and social change.

In the mid-1980s the relationship between staff members and the executive director had deteriorated. One month a staff person sent a letter of "no confidence" in the executive director to the board, and the executive director resigned shortly afterwards. In the aftermath of her sudden resignation staff were stunned and in shock. Two months later most of the board had resigned, and the organization descended into chaos. The agency counted on loyal insiders to help get through this time. One staff member said:

> It was like going home and finding out a family
> member was not there anymore. While trying to
> understand what happened, we still had to eat and

do everyday things. We were panic stricken and in a state of shock. It took months before we came up with the idea of a co-directorship and started to function again.

A letter from staff to agency volunteers read:

We are an organization that has experienced and permitted serious abuses of power, racism...we are not sure why this institutional disintegration has occurred.

The anxiety and turmoil, internal disintegration, and inability to function are consistent with characteristics of traumatization.

As is apparent from outside consultation two years later, the event and its aftermath were not sufficiently addressed and were continuing to negatively impact the agency's functioning. The external consultant found that board members still had unresolved feelings about the previous events.

The story of the transition that occurred two years earlier was a family secret. It was not openly discussed and...many board members did not know the story and were afraid to ask...The situation was exacerbated by the stories that the previous director allegedly had abused her power and that she had resigned after being confronted with this information. I believed that the fear of being accused of abusing power prevented board members from taking power at all (Green, 1989).

In the mid-1990s board-staff relationships began to fracture. This deterioration played out in written communication that expressed misunderstanding, hurt, and anger, and concerns about how to address the rift. The following statement in a letter (internal document, 1995) from the women of color on staff to the board exemplified the tenor and seriousness of the issues:

We feel that the interactions between the board
members and women of color staff represent a classic
example of the way in which racism affects our agency.

A second letter to the board (internal document, 1995), signed by all staff, showed continuing tension.

We believe that a deep chasm has developed between
the board and the staff that can only be lessened by
opening the doors of communication.

This chasm between the board and staff was not the only dysfunctional pattern occurring. During this time the co-directors' relationship was strained, and communication between the two of them stopped. Staff members felt confused and unsettled, and began to take sides. One staff summarized:

Something happened, and they were not working so
well together – the whole staff was aware of what was
going on.

At the end of the year the co-director, a woman of color, submitted her resignation effective several months hence. Four days later the board of directors fired her. The firing was the official, though not the public, story. Within several months, five additional staff resigned or were fired. One staff's letter of resignation indicated a "hostile, unhealthy work environment and unresolved intense feelings related to the co-director's firing and subsequent work atmosphere." In research interviews individuals described confusion and secrecy about the co-director's termination:

When [the co-director] disappeared, I heard about it
through various communities. It was hush-hush.

The co-director was gone. We heard that she was fired.
We were supposed to say that she was no longer at

*the agency. There was a lot of stress and we were not
dealing with it directly.*

Six months after the co-director was fired the organization was still in turmoil.

The organization engaged an external consultant to assist with the "healing and rebuilding process." Focused on understanding and moving through the conflict, the consultation did not heal the rifts between staff and board or those among staff. Staff who joined the agency after that period reported feeling heavily influenced by that conflict. New staff were encouraged by the executive director to read documents from that period and to talk with staff members who had been with the agency at that time. Said one woman:

*People were angry, bitter, and confused, and felt
unheard. It was like a dysfunctional family and no one
was allowed to talk about it.*

Staff of color who continued working at the agency reported feeling guilty for not resigning in solidarity with the fired co-director. The importance of insider relationships and the ambivalence about power and leadership led to intensifying and spreading the feelings. The vehicles for communicating feelings and spreading stress were overt; everyone was in conversation with co-workers. The dynamics of stress, anxiety contagion, and a sense of futility or depression evident in the descriptions undermined the agency's productivity and health.

Dynamics of racism, harmful rifts within the agency, and secrecy not addressed in the late 1980s intensified and deepened the hurt, anger, and feelings of helplessness in 1995. The inability of agency members to come together to talk about the traumatic events when they occurred left a variety of feelings associated with unresolved grief. The undercurrents of abuse of power, coupled with the historical ambivalence about power and leadership, exacerbated the immediate situations and increased the hurt and mistrust. That racism was a central part of both traumas added to the unaddressed experiences of racism and oppression in the agency. The layers of unresolved hurt and anger thickened and festered. Individuals resigned, but the feelings never left the agency.

The unhealed trauma of both events, coupled with the agency's organizational culture and unaddressed effects of cumulative trauma, set the stage for the dynamics in the last year of the entity's existence. The unaddressed traumatization had drained the agency's internal resources and left it in a precarious position when its long-time executive director departed.

Cascading Series of Re-traumatizing Events

The executive director, who had been there ten years, left to lead another nonprofit. After an unsuccessful search for a new executive director the board put in place an interim strategy. Over the next eight months staff, board, and external consultants filled the interim executive director role. Board members became increasingly distressed and discouraged, and individual staff members began to think about leaving.

By the end of that time the situation was rapidly deteriorating. The five-person board of directors was overwhelmed and seeking someone to save them from a difficult situation. Staff and board members described the situation:

> We cared about the organization — we were bright,
> but inexperienced good people...We were not
> functioning effectively.

> It was amazing how quickly I lost objectivity. I tried
> to stay clear of the chaos. I was like a rabbit in the
> headlights. I still carry that experience with me.

*The last year was filled with power struggles...tension
between the board and the staff... The board saw us
as troublemaking upstarts, young radicals who make a
fuss...There was resentment both ways.*

There was almost no communication between staff and board as they
blamed each other for the situation. Feelings of despair and hopelessness come through in these quotes. The agency's closed organizational
boundaries hampered it further. Few conversations occurred between
agency members and outsiders, and no one sought outside help for the
agency. Comments:

*It never occurred to me or any of us to ask for help, or
even that there was someone who could help.*

*We did not know whom to call for help. Abused staff
don't tell; they are enmeshed in unhealthy dynamics
and don't talk about it. We were in a trance state, like
hypnotized robots, not recognizing our choices.*

Insiders were lost in internal dynamics and cut off from help.

Shortly after arriving, the last interim executive director fired individual
staff, tightened control over internal structure and systems, and questioned the future of various programs. She disbanded the volunteer
staffing of the crisis line and negotiated its transfer to a sister agency.
At the same time remaining staff one by one began to resign. The
interim executive director brought up the agency's possible closure in
a discussion with the board. At that time she also asked for assistance
and ideas from external resource people but did not communicate
the imminence of the agency's closure. After a series of closed meetings the five-member board, in a three to two decision, voted to shut
the agency. The board rolled over. It had no emotional energy left.
Comments:

*It was weird how quickly it all happened, bizarre,
numbing, especially couched as a funding issue.*

It was like we were infected by a terrible cancer. The interim executive director said essentially we had no alternative.

These statements express the sense of despair and loss of hope.

The interim executive director brought together the primary funders to inform them of the closure, citing finances and possible liability issues. Many members of the community, including funders, were stunned and puzzled. Reasons given for the agency's closure left nearly everyone with unanswered questions. Several interviewees said their interview was their first significant conversation about the agency's end. A former staffer said, "When I heard the agency had closed, it was like hearing that someone had died." The abrupt finality short-circuited any collective acknowledgement of the closure, celebration of its history and contributions, and grieving of its loss. Whatever opinions they held about the agency's closure, the majority described the process of ending as unhealthy.

This rape crisis center closed because it lost its energy and hope through an interrelated set of factors that included: characteristics of organizational culture that added to trauma susceptibility; cumulative trauma from its empathic and redemptive work, particularly dynamics related to racism and anti-oppression; and the unhealed wounds from the two traumatizing events related to leaders' departures. The accumulated toll of these factors on the organization left it unable to cope with a rapidly deteriorating situation, re-wounding in itself, in the final months of its existence.

This chapter concludes the first section of the book. The three chapters of Part Two turn to ways to help organizations that have experienced some form of trauma. The next chapter focuses on assisting organizations recover and heal from the immediate aftermath of a traumatic occurrence and helping them avoid an outcome like that suffered by the rape crisis center.

6

INTERVENING IN THE IMMEDIATE AFTERMATH OF TRAUMA

An entity that experiences trauma may or may not become a traumatized system. Helping an organization to heal from a traumatic occurrence can prevent the system from becoming traumatized. By mitigating the negative impact of the trauma and enabling the organization to stabilize and heal itself, the organization is less likely to develop a traumatized culture.

In this chapter we discuss how to help an organization address the immediate aftermath of trauma. Chapter Seven explores ways to facilitate healing in an organization that has suffered from cumulative trauma or has a history of unhealed trauma. In Chapter Eight we focus on ways to pay attention to the dynamics and health of an organization's culture in order to discover and address harmful patterns before they compromise the organization's coping ability.

The chapter continues with a story from Pat's consulting practice. A pseudonym is being used to protect the identity of this organization.

The Helping Girls Abroad Story

Pat answered the phone one day and heard, "Do you have time to talk? I was told that you might be able to help us. We are in big trouble, and we do not know what to do. I am afraid this conflict is going to destroy our organization." This frantic executive director, who introduced herself as Ellen, was at the end of her rope. Ellen said she felt traumatized by the unfolding events. She thought her organization – a small grass-roots effort to support educational work with girls in another country – might fall apart if they did not get help to address the immediate situation. Ellen was distraught and worried that the situation threatened the organization and might even cause it to collapse.

As the conversation progressed, Pat discovered problems had been brewing and festering for at least a year. Peggy, a second staff person, had been spreading significant unrest among board members and some donors by speaking ill of the executive director and communicating a lack of confidence in her ability to lead. The negative energy was spreading beyond the borders of the organization and its reputation was at stake. Ellen felt betrayed and could no longer trust Peggy. She declared the relationship to be broken.

Some background is relevant. Thirteen-year-old Helping Girls Abroad (HGA) works to empower young women from extremely poor neighborhoods in a developing country by providing significant enrichment to their otherwise inadequate education. This enrichment increases their chances of going to university. Ellen, an American, founded the program in partnership with local leaders. Based on democratic principles with control in the hands of the local community members, the program thrived on passion and international support. But, it had little structure. HGA had three staff members who handled all operations in the United States. They tended to work informally without clearly delineated roles and responsibilities. The board of directors officially operated in the USA, with some of its members living overseas, and was comprised of well-meaning individuals who supported the mission and egalitarian values of the organization. The board also worked in an informal manner based on relationship, energy, and love of the program. Those involved were very proud of their work on behalf of the girls.

The informal administrative structure led to a situation in which each staff person was acting on her own understanding of what was needed for the organization and making decisions somewhat independently of the other. While Ellen traveled on behalf of the program or her individual research, Peggy applied for grants and set various events in motion. Eventually these two main staff found themselves with different ideas about their roles and collided in conflict that was neither explicitly addressed nor satisfactorily resolved. Ellen, self-admittedly conflict avoidant, knew something was wrong and felt uncomfortable enough to avoid conversation and interaction with Peggy. However, Ellen did not understand the depth of Peggy's frustration. Until board members were on the receiving end of Peggy's complaints, Ellen and the board members were unaware of how serious the situation had become. Ellen and the board officers were worried about negative comments being spread beyond the organization because they feared harm to the organization and its reputation. The officers did not know what to do to calm the situation down, but they were determined to support Ellen.

Pat agreed to help them figure out a reasonable way to deal with the situation as it was. In gaining more information, she discovered this organization operated with a lack of clarity about staff and board roles and almost no written policies. Loose structure and triangulated conversations left very unclear boundaries between board and staff and between the organization and wider community. Multi-directional conversations, including numerous international phone calls, also spread the stress very quickly. By the time Pat was in conversation with Ellen and board officers, many individuals were feeling the negative tension. One commented that the situation was very toxic and there seemed to be no way out of it.

Pat assumed the role of containment early on in her conversations. She listened and assured Ellen that they could find a way to address this situation without harming the organization. Whether clarifying tasks or boosting confidence, Pat was always conscious of alleviating client anxiety. It needed to be at a manageable level in order for organizational members to deal with the realities they faced.

Ellen decided she needed to ask Peggy to resign. Pat helped Ellen clarify her authority, and in a session with the executive committee, she helped clarify the role of the board in supporting the authority of the executive director. It became apparent that there were no policies in place to cover these circumstances. The officers recognized their responsibility and developed a strategy for addressing this situation at their upcoming board meeting. By the end of this session each felt appreciably more confident and less anxious. Pat agreed to be present at the board meeting as a resource person, but not in formal facilitator role.

Ellen was still unsettled about how to proceed with Peggy. Ellen was very nervous about asking for Peggy's resignation or even being in a direct conversation with her. Ellen was afraid she would not be able to hold her own in the face of Peggy's hostility. She and Pat talked through her feelings, and Pat communicated that she thought Ellen could handle this delicate situation. As with the board, Pat agreed to be at the meeting between Ellen and Peggy as a resource and support, but not in a formal mediator role. Jointly Ellen and Pat developed some talking points that Ellen could use and a contingency approach to the possible outcomes they could anticipate. At the end of the conversation Ellen was more hopeful but still not confident.

The board meeting and staff conversation were held one day apart. Pat saw her resource role in two ways: Holder of the space and content resource on issues related to board functioning and executive director functioning. Holding the space meant acting in a calm and non-judgmental way in the midst of others' anxieties and offering hopeful but realistic comments and energy to the conversation. These actions helped create a way for difficult feelings to be expressed and honest communication to occur. Pat wanted each person to leave with his or her dignity intact. In the board meeting Pat listened empathically to one board member who was teary with emotion from her surprise and dismay at the turn of events. Pat also made a number of comments about how well they had begun to handle the situation and how they were using their collective creativity and common sense to make decisions. She affirmed the choices the executive committee had made and advised them when they started to lose the clarity they had reached. Pat also shared other client circumstances in which board members had dealt with tough situations so these board members understood they were not alone in their experiences. As a content informant Pat explained the role a board usually played in this type of process and clarified the implications of decisions the board was considering.

Likewise Pat played a similar role in the meeting Ellen had with Peggy. That meeting had only two individuals but more intense interactions between them. Ellen, with coaching from Pat, communicated the board's decisions and also communicated her appreciation and support for Peggy's contributions to the organization. Peggy said she would resign after being told by Ellen that she would not be given the new role that she desired. They agreed to work together to ensure a calm transition for the organization. In keeping with her established pattern of conflict avoidance, Ellen did not delve into her staff person's actions. Neither did Peggy repeat any of her allegations about Ellen directly to her. Even with mostly tasks to discuss, feelings ran high enough to cause tears and breaks in the conversation. It did not seem to be a time for exploring the mutual hurt and pain. Perhaps at a future time, Ellen and Peggy could explore their relationship and what went awry, but in the midst of the crisis they needed to get through the immediate decisions.

After these meetings, it seemed that the organization was stabilized in the immediate aftermath of the trauma but that its future was still uncertain. Their fear and anxiety were lowered sufficiently so decisions for the organization could be made. One board member said Pat had taken a toxic, impossible situation and helped them see their way through it.

However, this was not the end of the turmoil. Within a couple of days, it became known that a key staff in the local community overseas was very upset. Hearing this second hand, Ellen immediately composed an email to announce her resignation. A board member strongly encouraged her to speak with Pat first. Pat encouraged Ellen to think about the ramifications of her action for the organization's sustainability. She also advised Ellen to speak to all board members before making this announcement public so they could be prepared for its aftermath. Ellen took Pat's guidance, and spoke with board members, who were shocked and said that this would be "the death of the organization". Ellen rescinded her sudden resignation. The board and Ellen agreed they would proceed with the severance package for Peggy and Ellen would start succession planning. When the organization was in a more stable situation, she would leave. Pat's role in these conversations was to help the executive director avoid making the situation worse.

Twice disaster was avoided, but the future of this organization was still uncertain. Had they gained enough confidence and learned enough about their roles to make this succession plan work? Would their relationships hold together through the transitions?

Traumatic Events and Traumatized Systems

This chapter covers situations in which the organization suffers a sudden disastrous event or a series of harmful events that destabilize the organization and make it susceptible to becoming a traumatized system, or in the worst circumstances, to failing completely. With or without any preexisting stressors, systems are shocked and severely wounded. The above example shows how a series of events can abruptly destabilize an organization and leave it unable to function. The deadly bombing in Oklahoma City and other instances of workplace or school violence are further examples of sudden devastating events. Whether the devastation comes from a single event or a series of events, the effects are unbearable and seriously threaten the organization. The immediate response to these events – recognizing and responding to the danger – influences how the organization copes, heals, and recovers and whether it suffers the enduring negative effects of a traumatized system.

Devastating events threaten the organization's very existence. It may be a threat to the physical structure, to its members' physical safety, or to the organization's economic security. Or it may be a psychological threat to the organization's self-esteem, its ability to take action, or its core identity. Any of these circumstances may be exacerbated if the organization has been suffering over time from serious stressors or cumulative traumatization. The rape crisis agency described in the previous chapter was already weakened by several unhealed historical traumas and an unrecognized pattern of cumulative organizational trauma. The events of its last year were the last straw. On the other hand, the violent attack on the women's health clinic described in the introductory chapter needed no pre-existing conditions to make it an organization-threatening event.

It is important to distinguish between suffering a devastating trauma and becoming a traumatized system. Many organizations suffer devastating traumas. Suicide of a leader, workplace or school shootings, death of a client, bombing of a building, sexual abuse of clients or staff, a catastrophic accident in which people are killed; the examples are numerous. As an individual may suffer trauma from a devastating event and recover with help from family and friends, an organization that suffers a traumatic event may recover through accessing internal and external resources. The individual and the organization both are in pain, suffer loss, grieve, and are vulnerable because of the catastrophe, but they can recover and do not necessarily experience a long-term impact that negatively re-orients their worldview.

However, some organizational traumas are so overwhelming and widespread that without significant intervention the system will become traumatized. In these circumstances the dynamics of trauma embed themselves in the culture of the system. In order to prevent this occurrence the dynamics must be recognized and addressed early. Otherwise, an organization closes down and turns in on itself with eventual shrinking of the energy available to heal and sustain the organization. Even with intervention these systems may still experience severe aftereffects and exhibit one or more characteristics of a traumatized system.

In other circumstances the event(s) may be devastating but more contained in scope and impact. Some members of the system close to tragic events may feel traumatized themselves and seek help, but the aftermath of the events does not spread throughout the organization and affect the culture as whole. For example, a staff member in one unit of a multi-unit youth-serving agency sexually assaulted a client. That unit's workers felt traumatized, and the executive managers responsible for safety throughout the organization reported feelings of trauma. Immediately those managers sought help for staff to talk through their experience and feelings. In addition the leaders speedily acted to address shortcomings in their policies and procedures to prevent a repeat occurrence. The organization learned from the experience and addressed the tragedy in a way that strengthened the organization itself. Organizational memory still holds the event but with little emotional charge, and the organization members do not act afraid of this kind of event happening again.

In either circumstance – widespread or contained – the system may become traumatized if it does not have internal or external resources to help alleviate the wounding and damage effectively. Sometimes, in the moment, no one understands the toll the devastating event is taking on the organization. So no one recognizes the potential for long-term negative impact. Since frequently individuals express the pain of a system, it may be that the focus is on individuals' abilities to cope and the systemic effect is missed. Other times leaders are not willing to face and explore the tragic events and so the organization has no vehicle for collective meaning making and healing.

The primary purposes of intervening in these kinds of traumatic situations are to aid the organization in healing from the event(s) and the damage caused and additionally to prevent the organization from turning into a traumatized system. For the health of the organization both purposes are crucial. How the organization deals with the immediate impacts will set the stage for whether the system becomes a traumatized system. How the organization moves forward after the initial healing occurs and what it learns from its experiences determine the organizational memory of the events and their influence on the organizational culture. While different actions support each purpose, they are intertwined; actions that support healing also help protect against a descent into traumatization.

Healing Process

Healing from organizational trauma is a process, and there are steps and tools of effective interventions. In the case of a devastating traumatic event, for an organization to heal and avoid long-term traumatization the following must be addressed:

- Ensure stability, safety, and containment

- Name the trauma and normalize experience

- Integrate the trauma in affirming and meaningful ways

- Move forward

Ensure stability, safety, and containment

Before healing can occur the organization needs help in stabilizing itself. It also needs help in recognizing and addressing dangers. The hurt and fear are so strong, the disorientation so complete, and the disbelief so pervasive that the organization cannot function in any normal sense. The first step is to witness the organization's experience – literally be present to show an awareness of its pain and tragedies. The second is to help an organization protect itself and assess its safety needs to prevent further harm. This may be assuring physical safety or it may be providing psychological haven or respite. Though the organization may not be able to function normally, it does need to be able to function at a minimal level. For example, in HGA, the executive director was caught up in her own emotions and worries. Both the board president and Pat helped her see the steps she needed to take to address the situation.

In order to help stabilize a group someone must provide a container that can hold the range of experiences and emotions present in those early moments. These containment actions may take hours or days. The actions are both stopgaps and first steps. They are stopgaps so the organization's response does not make the situation more tragic than it already is. In such situations there is a risk that the first responses are to "get on with things", to "get back to normal", or "hang tough and show them". By giving in to these attitudes the organization short circuits its own awareness and healing process. The resource person helps the organization see the need to step back and pay attention. In providing the container resource people are also acknowledging the actual state of affairs and recognizing that "things are not normal". Those attitudes support the organizational members themselves in their acceptance of the non-normal circumstances.

Any containment action is also one of the first steps in the healing process. At Helping Girls Abroad, Pat played a key role in alleviating the sense of helplessness by providing structure and positive confidence about the organization's ability to cope with the situation. She interrupted a downward spiral toward hopelessness. Helping the organization heal means helping it become whole again. At a minimum healing means a return to pre-trauma quality of functioning. At best healing strengthens the organization and leaves it at a higher level of functioning. In order to heal the organization the trauma needs to be recognized by its members as a systemic occurrence. Because the tendency is to see individual pain and fear, even individual inability to cope, the widespread impact on the fabric of the organization may be lost. Naming the experience collectively invites all members to come together and allows the organization to see itself as a whole. Ultimately this recognition builds organizational strength and power.

Name the trauma and normalize experience

Naming the trauma is a powerful step in healing and recovery. It helps to normalize the individual and collective responses happening in the organization. Shana and Pat have heard innumerable comments about the power of naming the trauma and the reactions. An executive director said to Pat, "I wish I had had this conversation with you four months ago, when I first took this job. What you are describing helps me now to make sense of my experience." In another conversation an individual recounted her pain at having to leave a social service job. "I thought that it was my fault that I could not cope with the dynamics. Now I see that the whole system was traumatized." In many highly mission-driven cultures norms about what is discussable and how conflict is managed prevent open conversation about painful topics. Ironically, despite the fact that many of these organizations support their clients' facing their traumas and painful experiences, the organizations do not do this for themselves.

In order to explore and understand the trauma's impact on the organization, the collective emotion and anxiety need to be held in a safe way. Allowing feelings to be expressed begins that process; the act of labeling what has only been swirling emotions or thoughts and amorphous anxiety helps bound the experience. As in HGA the leaders felt there was no way out of the situation. They needed to regain some confidence in their ability to respond carefully. Pat worked to contain their anxiety so it did not turn into precipitous steps while also helping them see themselves as capable of taking appropriate action. Paradoxically, organizational members need to be validated in the reality of their dreadful experience – it has been hard and it might still be hard for some time – and also encouraged to feel hope for the future, a sense that they will get to the other side of the pain and suffering.

A particular challenge occurs when a current traumatic event brings up memories and feelings of previous traumatic events. Sometimes this dynamic is exacerbated because those re-opened wounds are from previously unresolved (and potentially unacknowledged) traumas. The amount of emotion, bottled up for so long, erupts with a power that surprises everyone. This occurred in the rape crisis center described in the previous chapter. When the second leader left in the mid-1990s, the unresolved hurt and anger from eight years earlier resurfaced in dysfunctional ways.

Integrate trauma in affirming and meaningful ways

Once the emotion and anxiety are held in a safe way – this is an ongoing process, not a single conversation – organizational members can begin to listen to one another. By hearing each other, they begin to create a shared picture of their experience. Building on each other's perceptions of the traumatic event(s), they create a collective understanding of what happened to them and their organization. That understanding sets the stage for a process of making meaning and learning from the trauma both at the individual and the organizational levels. The meaning making is a construction of a collective reality, not a search for an external truth about the situation nor a process of convincing each other of some individual's believed truth. This last point is important because in times of extreme stress, interpersonal judgments and a need to blame individuals frequently emerge. These behaviors can further harm an organization already debilitated by the trauma. The point of an explicit meaning-making effort is to "re-member" (a way of making whole) a group that has been torn apart. It is literally a way to animate the group's collective mind and memory to deal with the tragic circumstances. If collective meaning making does not happen effectively, the worldview of an organization narrows or distorts. The distortion or narrowing compromise the organization's relationships with the outside world and limit the energy it needs for moving forward.

Move forward

After the organizational members have conversed sufficiently to reach some common conclusions, it is time to shift the energy to a more action-oriented framework. The traumatic event itself disrupted the organization's functioning in real and significant ways. Sometimes there are literally pieces to be picked up. Other times there are symbolic, but no less important, pieces. How will we stay safe in our most vulnerable time? How will we communicate with each other? How will we tell our organizational story to others? What is needed to support each other and make certain that individuals are being taken care of and getting what they need? How will we ensure that what we are doing is adding to the health and sustainability of the organization and limiting further damage? How can we accomplish the learning necessary while making sure the work of the organization carries on? Sometimes it is difficult to switch from the processing and learning mode to the action-oriented mode. The transition occurs in fits and starts as organizational members find themselves regressing back into a sea of emotions. Often it is hard to accomplish this shift without outside help.

Some organizations have adequate resources to accomplish the above tasks themselves, but others do not. Organizational leaders are in the best position to determine the adequacy of their resources. Paying attention to whether the organization is recovering on its own or sliding towards the characteristics of a traumatized system is an essential leadership function. It is also crucial that leaders notice when they have reached their individual limits of coping so they can ask for help. Making a determination to get help can be critical to the future health of the system. If the organization is awash with anxiety and not functioning, the leaders can ask for assistance from someone whose perspective is different from that of the organizational insiders. This person need not be a paid consultant, but he or she does need to be someone who can tolerate being immersed in others' intense emotions and anxieties.

In one example from our practice a board of directors fired the organization's executive director. This caused a wellspring of protest from the community served by this organization. The organization's credibility and reputation were on the line. Community leaders moved swiftly to contain the crisis by becoming involved with the board of directors and by offering resources to address the situation. In this case the organization's boundaries were never allowed to close down. It took almost a year for the organization to regain its functioning. The community leaders who intervened were essential in making that happen.

To be effective the responses described in this chapter need to be proportionate to the size and scope of the trauma. As in the example of a staff assaulting a client, the unit that experiences the trauma needs the support to get through it, but the whole organization may not need the same level of attention. On the other hand, a widespread organizational calamity, like a workplace killing or death of a leader, means the whole organization needs to be included in the response. Similarly an organization that is terrorized by a physical attack needs a different intensity and quality of response than does an organization wounded by a leader's embezzlement of resources. The deeper the intensity and the wider the impact the more human energy is needed to offer containment and structure. Any response needs to be tailored to fit the situation.

This chapter focused on dealing with the aftermath of devastating traumatic events. The purposes of the responses are to heal the organization and help it to avoid becoming a traumatized system. In the next chapter we turn our attention to providing assistance to organizations already experiencing the deleterious effects of traumatization. It describes how to help organizations recognize and address the impact of unacknowledged or unhealed trauma and how to deal with cumulative trauma embedded in the organization's culture.

7

INTERVENING IN ORGANIZATIONS WITH UNHEALED OR CUMULATIVE TRAUMA

Not all responses to traumatic events are adequate for healing an organization. In some circumstances the impacts from trauma go unrecognized; in other circumstances the trauma is recognized but the response is insufficient for healing. In this chapter we take up situations in which healing did not occur and the trauma became embedded in the organizational culture. We also cover discovery and response to cumulative trauma.

The organization might recognize the damage and acknowledge it but address the impacts in a superficial way. "We just need to get on with our organizational life." In other situations no one recognizes the trauma's occurrence in the moment. Aftereffects will surface in some later crisis or subsequent traumatic event. "I thought that we had dealt with that situation years ago. Why is it coming up now?" In both of these circumstances unhealed wounds and their impact become buried in the organization's culture, and the organization and its members suffer from this unacknowledged harm.

In other circumstances certain types of cumulative trauma develop and are incorporated into the organizational culture. These traumas almost always develop without organizational members realizing it. This out-of-awareness dynamic adds to the trauma's insidious character and powerful influence. In these situations recovery and healing depend on the organization's identifying the trauma.

We continue with a story from our organizational research to illustrate what it is like to uncover multiple kinds and severities of traumatization in an organization. The remainder of the chapter details an approach to helping an organization face its history and dynamics.

The Save Our Youth Story

The story of our research project with Save Our Youth (SOY) illustrates the intricacy of the discovery process and the intertwining aspects of traumatization. This organization requested anonymity, so details of its identity and circumstances have been masked. The executive director was interested in our conducting research on her organization as part of this book. In existence for almost forty years to serve at-risk youth, SOY appeared to be thriving after having come through a very difficult set of years. Perhaps this organization, with its experiences of trauma, could show ways an organization might survive a traumatic event and thrive? Pat and Shana led a group of researchers who set about contacting and interviewing members of the staff, board, and community who had worked in or with the organization over its four decades. The researchers presumed their exploration of the organization's culture would find indications of organization-wide trauma – the executive director had offered several examples – and evidence of how the organization had overcome those circumstances. The emerging picture and story turned out to be much more complicated, and interesting.

The researchers listened to stories about the culture and did indeed find examples of devastating traumatic events. However, they heard many stories that led them to identify ongoing patterns and evidence of other kinds of trauma: cumulative traumatization from the nature of the work and traumatization from internal dynamics.

Devastating events

Devastating events included the death of a client's baby in a pregnant teen program; the sexual assault of a resident by a staff member and the subsequent halt to placement of youth in the program; and the sudden closure of its main crisis shelter due to economic challenges. The organization responded to these events in ways that enabled the entity to face the pain and suffering of staff and clients and strengthen the organization at the same time. For example, in the program for pregnant teens immediate debriefing and counseling from outside professionals was offered to staff to help them cope in the short term. In another example, when the rape of a shelter resident was reported to organizational leaders and law enforcement, the organization's top managers quickly took steps to offer debriefing and counseling opportunities for staff and to put in place policies that ensured such a tragedy could not occur again. Through such a thorough and quick response they assured state personnel that children could safely be placed in the shelter again. Because of their actions the state agency's order to stop placement lasted only three days. In the example of the emergency shelter's closure, the organization went public with the action and garnered significant support in lobbying the city for more money to open another facility. They succeeded in regaining their lost funds. Each of these events and subsequent actions showed the organization had the capacity to respond appropriately to traumatic occurrences and to avoid the negative effects of such events becoming embedded in the organization's culture.

Cumulative trauma

We began to see patterns of cumulative traumatization that arose from the empathic nature of the organization's work. One pattern was a pendulum swing between hope and despair from contact with youth in desperate and dangerous conditions. Staff and volunteers remembered specific youth – their tragedies and their transformations and the devastation they felt when a youth committed suicide. They expressed their hope for all youth while working with individuals who failed again and again in their quest for stability and success. As one person said, staff demonstrated a saintly dedication to saving the youth.

Services included meeting youth on the streets where they gathered and accepting the youth as they were. This approach set the stage for a pattern of staff over-identifying with youth and blurring professional boundaries. One staff member said he practically lived on the streets with the youth – he was downtown every night. Another commented that staff emulated the negative aspects of homeless youth life, its manic and reactive culture. "It was like waiting for the next disaster and then jumping in to fix it." Young staff members who were dealing with their own issues seemed drawn to "youth on the brink."

Cumulative trauma also came from the redemptive nature of SOY's work. SOY staff worked in the midst of wider community indifference and frequent hostility toward runaway youth. Organizational members saw society as untrustworthy because it was hypocritical towards the youth and adversarial towards the organization's mission. SOY vowed to protect these young people from uncaring adults. This effort often meant operating at the edge of the legal system and out of the eye of the police during the period when a minor's running away was an illegal act. One program director said staff members were happy thwarting police. Staff were also encouraged to develop "antennae" to notice adults exploiting vulnerable children. These attitudes persisted and often left staff feeling despondent about the circumstances of "throwaway youth". These empathic and redemptive sources of cumulative trauma stressed the organization's culture and weakened it.

Internal wounding

In addition to cumulative trauma the researchers uncovered a number of events and decades-long patterns that seemed to indicate internal organizational wounding. Internal processes, relationships, and treatment of staff harmed individuals and created patterns of harm in the agency. These included:

- Historical pattern of ambivalent feelings and low-level hostility towards authority

- Personality-driven leadership style, described as a "cult of personality"

- Blurred boundaries, close friendships and intimate relationships

- Expendable staff who were paid low wages and suffered from job insecurity and high turnover

Historical pattern of ambivalent feelings and low-level hostility towards authority

The pattern of ambivalence and low-level hostility towards those in authority began early and continued through the decades. Whether in the 1970s or the 2000s, staff reported distance from and distrust of leaders and mixed feelings about leadership. Not everyone felt the same about an individual leader, especially with regard to executive directors, but patterns of tension about the roles of leaders and the place of authority in the system persisted. Working with adolescents likely influenced the staff and cultural perspectives on authority and leadership. Many staff identified with runaway youth who were badly treated by legal authorities and other adults. A number of staff were young, just out of their own teen years. This over-identification exacerbated the negative reaction to authority and distrust of leadership.

Personality-driven leadership style

Leaders influenced others through strength of personality and mission inspiration; loyalty was expected and rewarded. A key leader, usually the executive director, was at the center of organizational life. Everyone related to that leader, positively or negatively. Leaders interpreted the mission of the organization and acted on their interpretations. They chose directions for the organization according to their own preferences and interests. This authoritarian leadership style substituted for a rational strategic planning process. It resulted in expenditures of time, energy, and money not always in service to the core mission.

This leadership style also substituted for a clearly articulated and shared organizational structure and system of accountability and left staff with neither transparent process nor employment protection. Treatment of staff seemed to vary according to the quality of a staff member's relationship with the leader. If the leader liked the staff person, he or she was rewarded with praise and status and allowed leeway when performance concerns were raised. On the other hand, if the leader disliked the staff person, he or she was not treated well and given no leeway when concerns arose. Interviewees described these circumstances as unfair and demoralizing. Even though leaders were long gone from SOY, current staff expressed feelings about them with passion and vehemence.

Blurred boundaries, close friendships and intimate relationships

Patterns of blurred boundaries and close personal relationships among staff, board, and volunteers also persisted through the decades. Interviewees recounted sexual relationships among co-workers, partying that invited crossing professional boundaries, and personal friendship and antipathies that heavily colored staff interactions. These relationship patterns intensified staff perceptions of leaders playing favorites.

Expendable staff

Expendability of staff seemed to be an experience across the decades. They were paid low wages and suffered from job insecurity and high turnover. Staff members were allowed to operate and struggle independently, to do the best they could with the resources at hand, and to sink or swim on their own. It was accepted that staff would burn out and leave. The researchers surmised the staff members were treated by the agency as the youth were treated by society, that is, as expendable or "throw away". In one conversation a staff person labeled her experience as "being groomed" by an organizational leader, for what she was not sure. She made the direct connection between grooming street youth by exploitive adults and how she was treated as a young inexperienced staff person.

This "expendability" pattern was reinforced by the separate nature of the programs, by favoritism shown by leaders, by the fragmented and siloed nature of the culture, and by the lack of uniform structure and standards for supervision and professional development. Yet absolutely everyone interviewed expressed passion to serve vulnerable youth. This contradiction resulted in many staff and volunteers feeling ambivalent about their experiences – intensely alive and grateful for the opportunity to work with young people and used up and exhausted by the organization.

"The Dark Days"

One specific eighteen-month period during an interim executive director's tenure was described as "the dark days." It left many insiders with unhealed wounds and the whole organization in dire straits. The severe wounding of the organization was known and recognized by many in the organization, but was never addressed in a way that healing could occur. According to many staff interviewees, this period seemed to traumatize much of the organization. Individuals who were involved during that period described their pain and the pain of others as if it happened yesterday rather than many years earlier. In our opinion the organization still had not healed several years later at the time of our research.

Board leaders had a different perspective of that eighteen-month period. They either believed that staff members and leaders were incompetent or that one particular leader misled the board. They did not see a board role in the distress felt by many. Even as staff objections and concerns mounted during this time, board leaders failed to recognize the extent and intensity of the pain. A bad situation was exacerbated by the lack of board members' attention to the pain and lack of caring response from them while it was happening.

The residue from that eighteen-month period included significant distrust of leaders, lack of faith in the organization's administration, broken professional and personal relationships, and individual emotional pain and anger. The residue seemed similar to what we heard in our research about the rape crisis center.

SOY research summary

We expected our research to show how an organization healed and recovered from several devastating events in its history and to provide some information about how that had occurred. We discovered that healing from certain devastating events had, in fact, occurred. The organization had shown itself able to notice devastating trauma in the moment and take constructive action. However, that was not the complete picture. In addition to that healing, we heard many stories of pain and suffering from internal dynamics and saw some evidence of cumulative traumatization from the organization's redemptive and empathic work. In addition we recognized the traumatizing nature of the interim executive director's eighteen-month tenure. While SOY had shown itself to be competent to deal effectively with crises, it had failed to pay attention to troubling patterns. We concluded that this organization was a traumatized system and that it still needed to heal and build a healthy organizational culture.

Complexity of Traumatization

Devastating events by their nature demand attention. Though some organizations might not deal with these circumstances effectively, traumas are strongly felt. In addition actions committed by external sources are also relatively easy to see and acknowledge. On the other hand internal wounding from dysfunctional dynamics or empathic or redemptive work bores into an organization's culture in insidious ways. The organization's cultural rationales and defenses make it very difficult to see the harm.

In the remainder of this chapter we discuss the complexity of unhealed trauma and cumulative traumatization, ways to uncover these patterns, and strategies for building a healthy organization.

Traumatization in organizations can come from an interwoven set of healed historical traumas, unhealed historical traumas, internal wounding from longstanding organizational dynamics (cultural patterns), and cumulative trauma from empathic and redemptive work. The complexity and interwoven nature of these patterns make it easy to miss the complete picture.

The sum of the patterns is historical and current, widespread and confined, deeply hidden and just below the surface, personal and professional, and denied and remembered. These patterns and specific instances are uncovered by looking at the whole system from multiple perspectives. Looking at one part of the system might lead to a misunderstanding of what was really going on. Success in healing one unit may make it harder to recognize less obvious fallout in the rest of the organization. For example, SOY staff and residents were given opportunities to heal from the baby's death in the teen mothers program, but the program was eventually closed. Organization-wide fallout from that closure was not reported by any of the interviewees. Perhaps most staff felt relief from the visible organizational response to the trauma itself.

Focus on individuals as the main actors in a situation misses the deeper patterns at play. Leaders think individual's pain is unfortunate, but nothing can be done about it. Individuals leave the organization and the belief is "the problem" is gone. In addition to targeting individuals as the problem leaders might also see the problem as one department's rather than a wider pattern. No one notices how organizational structure, process, and cultural patterns cause harm. Interviewees from all decades described this pattern; it was most poignant in the hurt expressed by those who left under the interim director's tenure. No one saw the larger pattern of ineffective board leadership, lack of protective structures, and personality-driven decision-making.

The big picture might also be clouded by keen attention to one trauma or one dysfunctional pattern while failing to notice contributing patterns of historical influences. In certain circumstances overlapping events and patterns might include an unhealed trauma from a devastating event for one unit of a larger system and other cumulative patterns across the whole system. Discerning multiple factors and dynamics creates a richer and more realistic picture of the organization and what needs to be done to help it heal. Though many staff experienced painful relationships with one or more leaders and acknowledged historical tensions about leadership and authority at SOY, no interviewee made the connection between their specific circumstances and larger organizational patterns. Nor did they make reference to any parallels between the challenges of adolescence and the crises of runaway youth and the organization's challenges and crises.

An organization can continue to function without addressing these occurrences and patterns, but the presence of unacknowledged traumatization will make transitions in the organization's lifecycle more difficult. Leadership transitions, for example, seem to prompt organizational anxiety; unacknowledged and unhealed wounds intensify that anxiety. Often these transition times surface previously unidentified and unacknowledged patterns. Also, if there is unhealed trauma, an organization cannot be sure of its capacity to cope with future crises or increasingly stressful, even dire, environmental influences. The stories of WROC and the rape crisis center both showed that unaddressed traumas debilitated the agencies' abilities to face crises and contributed to their demise.

Recognizing and Acknowledging Traumatization

Coming to the realization that an organization has been affected by trauma and may be traumatized can happen in a number of ways:

1) an individual can be exposed to the ideas of organizational trauma and with this increased awareness begin to see patterns and symptoms in his or her organization; 2) a leader can undertake an organizational assessment for purposes of strengthening the organization or planning for the future and discover unexplainable and/or disturbing patterns; 3) patterns may erupt into harmful actions during a crisis and prompt organizational soul searching; or, 4) an external resource person, working with the organization, may notice patterns or symptoms that merit further attention. The SOY executive director was familiar with the ideas of organizational trauma and intrigued by what she might learn about her organization.

Often past situations or current patterns have been ignored or have been relegated incorrectly to a category of "history" or "finished business." Whatever the etiology or sources of patterns and whoever is involved, the first step for the organization is noticing something. What is going on at the organizational level? How can the collective see what has been ignored or denied? How can it be vulnerable enough to see beyond strengths and successes? The next step is making sense of what has been noticed. Is the system traumatized? Is there some other explanation for what has been discovered? (We are not suggesting all problems in an organization arise from organizational trauma, but rather some persistent negative influences may be from unhealed traumatization.) The process of recognition and acknowledgement includes creating enough safety for everyone to tell their story and be heard; recognizing the trauma or traumatization and naming the sources; and making collective sense of the discoveries.

In order to recognize and assess the situation members of the organization need a safe enough space to share their experiences and an individual or individuals to contain the anxiety present in that process. In order to create a safe enough space leaders need to prepare themselves for the revelations and subsequent reactions and feelings. They have to set aside their own defensiveness and confront their vulnerabilities and secrets. Sometimes leaders have already recognized clear signs of traumatization in their organization. If they have not, their preparation necessitates recovering from their own surprise and dismay at this discovery. Leaders need to create a safe space where each person's experience can be shared without interference from anyone else. Adequate preparation sets the stage for the next level of discussion that occurs with the whole organization. (Chapter Nine focuses specifically on the role of leaders and their experiences.)

Speaking and listening to each other leads to naming the specific traumatizing experiences. Understanding the characteristics of traumatized systems can help individuals describe their experiences. A group story begins to emerge from the collective sharing and discussing. That story helps answer the question: Is our organization experiencing a significant number of the characteristics of a traumatized system?

After realizing these characteristic patterns are occurring, organizational members are ready to explore the sources of their trauma. Each source of trauma has challenges associated with its detection and acknowledgement. For example, when looking for unhealed trauma, patterns of dis-ease in the system are signals. Negative and harmful behaviors and dynamics persist despite other organizational changes. If those behaviors and dynamics are associated with a particular time in the organization's history, they could be signs of unhealed trauma. Noticing these patterns and effects could lead to an exploration of the organization's history to uncover devastating events. Members can then assess whether or not those events were sufficiently addressed for the organization to heal.

Sometimes an organization, though stabilized, lingers at a compromised level of functioning with costs in productivity and health. For example, over-protectiveness and loss of trust in the community almost always come from the residue of devastating events perpetrated by outsiders. Consider the cost to the women's healthcare provider described in the introductory chapter. It instituted strong security systems and created a culture in which the attack was acknowledged annually.

Remembering the trauma kept it alive in the organization's culture and resulted in a "lasting psychic impact on the fabric of the organization." Such responses perpetuate a traumatized system. Leaders or members might later suspect sufficient healing had not occurred and the organization was still traumatized. Exploring that possibility under these circumstances could be tender. The organizational leaders, as in this example, might not see the collective actions as continuing the traumatization. Leaders may have done what they thought best to get the organization back on its feet and missed enduring signs of organizational harm.

Discerning traumatization from internal wounding also demands sensitivity to the situation. Most organizational dynamics develop and operate covertly. In order to surface patterns caused by internal wounding, members need a framework or structure to see the organization as a whole system. Otherwise a common reaction is to blame individuals for the dynamics. For example, in Save Our Youth, the tension around leadership led to staff blaming leaders for organizational ills and leaders blaming others for those same ills. The pattern of "leadership by personality" would be easy to miss. Laying responsibility for negative events at the feet of a particular leader ignores the underlying dynamics that enabled leaders to act on their own beliefs and inclinations rather than the organization's welfare.

Unrecognized cumulative trauma from empathic or redemptive work is perhaps easier to acknowledge. By definition it transcends the behavior of individuals and suggests some of the patterns come with the work itself. Many organizational members have been exposed to ideas about secondary traumatic stress, vicarious traumatization, compassion fatigue, and trauma stewardship. However, even with knowledge of these ideas it might be hard to accept that patterns exist at the organizational level and persist over time.

As the sources of trauma are uncovered, members have an opportunity to acknowledge their own and others' suffering and the impact of these experiences on organizational life. Collective meaning making is a powerful process because it allows what have been individual stories of pain, anger, fear, grief, and loneliness to become an organizational story. This is essential for the organization as a whole to accept its reality and be able to address that reality without blame or judgment of individuals. An understanding of the sources and dynamics of traumatization can help provide words and containers for this process. In a situation with multiple dynamics occurring, it is important to discuss and come to agreement about which aspects are the most important or urgent. Then steps to address the dynamics can be developed.

Addressing Organizational Traumatization

Identifying and agreeing on actions to address trauma through interventions specific to the sources, extent, and severity of the traumatization come next. Strategies are:

- Create processes for organization-wide dialogue and learning

- Remember organizational history and alleviate organizational amnesia

- Strengthen core identity and build organizational esteem

- Institute facilitating structures and processes

- Open system to outside energy and information

- Institute ways to nurture organizational spirit and engage in renewal

Not all of these strategies are relevant to every circumstance, but they provide a basic array of tactics to help the organization heal and become healthier. The basic approach and structure of providing safety and containment as well as opportunities for collective dialogue is essential in this phase of the work. All of these strategies could be useful to a healthy organization as well, but they are critical to a traumatized system trying to regain its health. Discussion of each of these strategies follows with examples from SOY.

Create processes for organization-wide dialogue and learning

Since one of the primary complications of organizational traumatization is mistaking an individual dynamic for an organizational dynamic, it is essential that an organization have a way to bring its members together to create a shared perspective about its reality. Unless the reality is constructed together, the organization runs the risk of having a picture of itself dominated by those with self-interest or insufficient understanding. Creating a shared perspective also provides opportunities to recognize changes and mourn losses that are inevitable in organizational life. For example, the executive director of SOY could have brought upper management and board members to hear a presentation by the researchers. Such a meeting could have started an open dialogue about organizational patterns and tested readiness for sharing with the full agency.

Remember organizational history and alleviate organizational amnesia

Creation stories and moral narratives are powerful elements of an organization's culture. They bind individuals to each other and to the work and form the basis for ongoing dialogue about organizational growth and development. Ongoing dialogue helps members and leaders recall historical challenges and successes and look ahead to the future. For example, a conversation among SOY board members about the interim executive director's tenure might have jogged individuals' memories of that time and prompted more honest recalling of circumstances and events.

Strengthen core identity and build organizational esteem

An organization's identity and culture allow it to function in its environment and create the foundation for its health and sustainability. Continual renewal of an organization's purpose, mission, and vision sustains its core identity and energizes its systems and people. Asking questions that help the organization stay realistic about itself, its reach, and its limits assures that the entity's self-perceptions stay rooted in a pragmatic analysis. Facing opportunities and challenges enables the organization to reaffirm its present effectiveness and create its future work. Open dialogue about staff experiences at SOY could have illuminated feelings of exploitation and perhaps encouraged the leadership to tackle the problems of low pay and high turnover. Reversing these patterns would have boosted staff morale and collective esteem.

Institute facilitating structures and processes

Many organizations face the challenges of providing enough structure and process to support organization growth and maturation. In traumatized systems that development might have been short-circuited early in the organization's history. Or it could have been stalled as the organization protected itself or distorted because of dysfunctional internal dynamics. As an organization heals and strengthens itself, it can look critically at its internal functioning. It is then able to decide which strengths to affirm, which norms to change, which structures to bolster, and which new processes to institute. These steps are essential for installing healthy process in the organization's culture. For example, Save Our Youth could begin to mitigate the history of personality-driven leadership by creating a transparent planning process and training its board of directors on roles and responsibilities. Leaders could ease employee fears about job security through honest conversations about programs and funding levels and allay the feelings of exploitation by committing to salary scales commensurate with peer agencies and instituting an organization-wide program on trauma stewardship.

Open system to outside energy and information

Traumatized systems have closed boundaries that end up isolating the organization from outside ideas and influences, even from like-minded allies. Overcoming this tendency takes courage because an organization might have to reach out when it is most vulnerable. Regular interactions with allies and community members help the flow of ideas and support. Convening discussions helps generate innovative perspectives and approaches to problems. Healthy relationships with other organizations assure help and support when it is needed. Since organizational depression is also a characteristic of traumatization, these strategies are doubly important. Outside sources keep the energy for the mission high and provide support for healing. Save Our Youth had a certain amount of "we can do this by ourselves" attitude throughout its history and an entrenched pattern of separation. It could have committed to developing alliances and partnerships as part of its strategic plan.

Institute ways to nurture organizational spirit and engage in renewal

Many highly mission-driven organizations have institutionalized ways to support staff renewal. However organizations often have no ways to focus on the spirit and essence of the organization as a whole. Infused with energy from a wider source and embedded in a system of organizational peers, organizations can weather difficult times and ask for help more easily. Many organizations have had practices to stay healthy but discontinued them, sometimes due to the very traumas that need to be healed. In those cases the challenge might be to reinvigorate past actions. SOY already takes an action that nurtures its spirit. It puts on an annual event that brings together hundreds of community members to hear youths' stories and demonstrate support for the organization.

This chapter focused on less obvious instances of organizational traumatization and ways to notice and address them. Most of the situations of insidious traumatization are complex and challenging because they have continued and deepened without being noticed. In the next chapter we focus on organizations that might be at risk from traumatization and are looking for ways to remain healthy and to be strong enough to cope with sudden traumatic events and other kinds of organizational challenges.

8

PAYING ATTENTION TO ORGANIZATIONAL PATTERNS

Though many highly mission-driven organizations do not suffer from current or unhealed traumas, their cultures are still influenced by the nature of their work. Many have enduring cultural effects related to the organization's creation or may be at risk for cumulative trauma. Even in the most positive situations, where there is no evidence of trauma, it is important for organizations to pay attention to their internal workings. For an organization's health and sustainability, its members have to be able to see the organization clearly, to pay attention to enduring patterns and emerging dynamics, and name systemic facets that need to be addressed.

The purpose of this chapter is to help highly mission-driven organizations avoid the pitfall of traumatization by understanding their organizational cultures, seeing patterns that may speak to deeper unresolved issues, and addressing normal dynamics to keep the organization strong. This exploration may be motivated by various factors. An organization may be in transition with leadership changes. The organization's growth might necessitate advancement to the next stage of its development, and it may need to increase its internal capacity. Or an external force could be putting pressure on the organization or creating disturbance in the organization's life.

Organizational leaders may want or need a deeper understanding of the organization and their roles. They may recognize certain repeating patterns or behaviors or suspect that the best collective work is not happening. There may be an underlying sense of malaise or atmosphere of unexpressed feelings. Leaders may need to address those covert elements or tap into the spirit of an organization.

Recognizing clues or symptoms in the system and naming what is occurring are the first steps to understanding the culture's influence on mission achievement and organizational health. Leaders and members need a framework and language for paying attention to what is occurring in the organizational culture. When they can focus on the whole entity, group members can see strengths, shadows, dynamics, behaviors, and patterns in their system. Without a framework organizations suffer because members cannot find ways to talk with each other about patterns of behavior that are occurring, but they nonetheless remain stuck in those patterns.

Organizational Patterns

Patterns make up organizational culture. Three kinds of patterns exist (Schein, 1994): Artifacts, espoused values, and basic underlying assumptions, all of which must be understood in relationship to each other. Taken together they create the web of understanding that binds each organizational member to every other in defined and undefined ways. Organizational patterns develop in conscious and unconscious ways and likewise are transmitted through explicit and implicit means.

Artifacts are the visible organizational structures and processes that are discussed, honored, and changed over time. Frequently leaders and followers alike tout these patterns as emblematic of the organization's identity. For example, new employees receive orientation and training about the visible and well-acknowledged aspects of culture, mission statements are displayed prominently on letterhead, and annual reports or web sites contain a brief history of the organization and mark changes in its development. These aspects are relatively easy to see and discuss.

Espoused values are also relatively easy to discern and discuss. These are the strategies, goals, philosophies, and stated values of the organization. Frequently they are communicated in the orientations mentioned above. Some documents, hung on the walls in view of clients and staff, convey the official messages of the organization. Though the messages appear to be universal, sometimes day-to-day business communicates another set of values. These "values-in-use" are experienced in less explicit ways and often become part of the third kind of pattern, underlying assumptions.

Underlying assumptions are the unconscious, taken-for-granted beliefs, perceptions, thoughts and feelings present in the organizational culture. Individuals learn these aspects of organizational culture in indirect and subtle ways. The existence of these patterns is hard to imagine and recognize. For example, without even realizing it, new staff use the language of their coworkers to describe their own experiences. Those words begin to shape the new staff members' thoughts and feelings.

Organizational members may experience uneasiness or confusion in response to any of the artifacts, espoused values, values-in-use, and underlying assumptions. Since much of this material is left unacknowledged and undiscussed and since organizational members typically do not recognize the patterns, they lack words to grasp and describe their experience. In many cases they have been socialized and trained to notice individual characteristics and behaviors, so their focus turns to specific individuals when "something is not right." Attention is placed on others' behaviors as the cause of uneasiness or confusion rather than on the group or organizational experience.

For example, in the rape crisis center's story the authors described reports about the abuse of power by several of the agency's executive directors. Those perceived abuses of power resulted in structural shifts to guard against future abuse.

Oscillation between co-director and executive director
governance structures became the norm. When a

leader left, the agency questioned its satisfaction with the structure in place and re-designed its governance. This questioning and re-design seemed to be a way that the agency as an organization played out its ambivalence about power and leadership. <u>Because the organizational members could not see the underlying organizational ambivalence with power, they could not see that the pattern was bigger than the behavior of the departing leader</u> (Underline added) (Hormann and Vivian, 2004, p. 10).

In order to "see" or "hear" patterns organizational members as a unit need to be able to pay attention to multiple factors, see behaviors in their context, and make connections among various parts. Effective organizational learning is collaborative in nature; it relies on the participation of individuals with multiple perspectives to offer. The sum total of each individual's recognizing a pattern is not the same as those individuals recognizing the pattern together, and individual insight about a group is not the same as the group's collective insight about itself. Shared recognition and collective meaning-making enable an organization as a whole to see itself clearly and to choose what to change.

Strengths and Shadows Model

Building on years of research and consultation with not-for-profit organizations, the authors developed the Strengths and Shadows Model to enable organizational members to move beyond a focus on individuals or interpersonal relationships and create an understanding of the organization as a whole system. This model provides an approach that interrupts blaming individuals for systemic issues and relieves the sense of being judged. It allows organizational members to discover historical and current patterns and to deepen their understanding of the organization's environmental context.

The model is based on an understanding that both strengths and shadows occur in organizational life. Strengths come from organizational qualities and values that are highly regarded by the internal environment, and for this reason they are usually visible. Explicitly, they are incorporated into value statements, policies, standards of practice, and recognition and reward systems. Shadows are often hidden aspects of the qualities and values. They develop through emerging interpersonal dynamics and implicit agreements about collective norms. Sometimes the shadows are a repository of aspects that are uncomfortable, denied, or discounted.

Both strengths and shadows are part of the organizational culture. They arise from choices about where to focus attention, how to respond to crises, and deliberate and/or inadvertent role modeling by leaders. Cultural contradictions emerge from values competing with each other, making conflict a given in organizational life. Organizational members develop rationales to account for these contradictions. Over time both contradictions and rationales become part of "what we just don't talk about around here." In order to see the organization as a whole, it becomes important to find a way to look beyond dynamics that seem like interpersonal (or personal) differences or values conflicts. In order to see the whole organization in relationship to its community it becomes essential to surface and own organizational qualities so they are not projected onto the wider environment.

For example, the leadership group of a broad-reaching anti-poverty organization was interested in strengthening its role and performance. With the use of the Strengths and Shadows Model the group constructed a picture of its organizational culture and reflected on the patterns that surfaced. They began to discern patterns, such as separation among programs and fragmentation of effort, that were not beneficial for the organization as a whole. By discussing the patterns they were able to see ways that improvement in their collective leadership behavior could shift these dynamics and strengthen the organization.

Understanding the Strengths and Shadows Model

The Strengths and Shadows Model offers one way for organization members collectively to see patterns and describe their culture. Members identify organizational Strengths and Shadows and gain an understanding of the relationships between the two. These are depicted on a graphic template that spatially arranges Strengths in an inner circle and Shadows in an outer circle with arrows connecting the related Strengths and Shadows. These discoveries give organization members the opportunity both to accept the qualities of their organizational culture and to focus on aspects they want to change. In doing so, they gain ownership of their own change process.

Figure 8.1. Social Changers

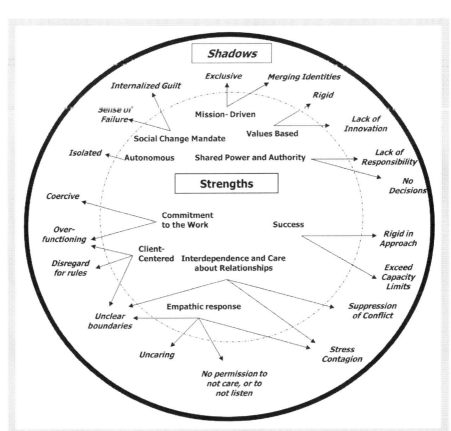

Using the Strengths and Shadows Model

Identification and description can begin with either Strengths in the inner circle or Shadows in the outer one. The process is finished when each Strength and Shadow has at least one counterpart in the other circle. As Figure 8.1 shows, a single Strength might have several Shadows and vice versa. When the group has completed naming and connecting the Strengths and Shadows, it reflects on the overall image and shares insights and meaning. This is an opportunity for the group to accept this picture of itself; once that happens, they can discover and begin to name organizational patterns. Discovering and naming those patterns helps members to comprehend their organization as a system. Recognizing strengths and shadows as organizational characteristics interrupts the tendency mentioned earlier to see individuals as "troublesome" or the source of problems. Based on organizational context and need the group identifies three or four patterns to explore further.

Social Changers example

We use the composite nonprofit "Social Changers" (see Figure 8.1) to show how an organization can use the Strengths and Shadows Model to learn about itself. This composite is drawn from numerous conversations with leaders and members of not-for-profit organizations.

In the Social Changers' graphic the pairing of the Strength *Interdependence and Care about Relationships* with the Shadow *Suppression of Conflict* suggests that these qualities exist together in the group, a contrast to labeling an individual or the group as conflict avoidant. It suggests a more nuanced understanding of these interpersonal dynamics. This shift in focus lessens blame and faultfinding and offers a more compassionate and hopeful foundation for making choices about change.

Additional examples from the Social Changers offer more detail about how this model works. Social Changers' staff members identify *Client Centered* to be a Strength and recognize three Shadows associated with that Strength: *Disregard for Rules, Over-Functioning,* and *Unclear Boundaries*. In discussion they see how these Strengths and Shadows connect with each other and play out. Staff self-consciously remember comments about how much they hate reporting requirements and how they'd prefer to be advocating for their clients (*Disregard for Rules*). As they continue the discussion, they realize that underneath their comments is an opinion that they know better than their funders what services their clients really need. They also explore *Over-Functioning* – their long hours, extra tasks, and going the extra mile for their deserving clients. As they dig more deeply into this aspect, they realize they are trying to reinforce the importance of their efforts and make up for their clients being mistreated in the past. With prompting from their leader, who has given this dynamic some thought, a couple of staff recognize that there might also be issues around boundaries (*Unclear Boundaries*). One staff member surfaces an important underlying assumption through her comment, "Sometimes we advocate so strongly for what our clients want that we forget we are employees of this agency. We end up over-identifying with the clients and disregard other responsibilities." These exchanges enable staff collectively to develop important insights.

Once these insights have surfaced, organizational members talk about what needs to change. With the realization that they can use light-hearted humor to change their attitude about reporting (*Disregard for Rules*), and an honest acknowledgement that they are hesitant to tackle the issues of *Unclear Boundaries*, the group decides to begin working on the shadow of *Over-Functioning*. They explore how their work inadvertently encourages them to over-identify with clients and talk about how to balance their client-centered approach with setting reasonable expectations for the agency as a whole. Staff also agree to call out subtle expectations about saying yes to overwork. While they recognize the importance of acknowledging their efforts and achievements, they begin to see that their individual over-functioning has a parallel of organizational over-functioning. Sustainability at both levels needs to be considered. Towards the end of this conversation their leader reminds them that they still need to address the Shadow of *Unclear Boundaries* and suggests that getting outside help for the team as a whole might be a good idea.

On another day staff articulate *Mission-Driven* to be a Strength with two Shadows: *Merging Identities* and *Exclusivity*. They are very proud they have stayed true to their mission despite the ups and downs of funding and community support and acceptance. As they talk about how proud they are, they begin to realize their own sense of who they are as professionals is closely tied to the success of the organization's mission and its part in the larger social change movement (*Merging Identities*). Some admit that work is the center of their lives. Again, with prompting from their leader, individuals begin to realize that their self-worth and self-esteem are tied up with the social change movement. In fact, a couple of staff say that they feel called to the work and cannot imagine working anywhere else; leaving the agency would be abandoning the cause. That opens the door for further reflection about what "calling" means in terms of work-life balance and their expectations of each other.

Looking at the second Shadow, *Exclusivity*, some staff remember comments from a meeting they had with individuals with disabilities and begin to see how their approach might not communicate sensitivity or respect for members of that community. These are unsettling thoughts because their approach works well with lots of their constituents. They acknowledge their underlying belief that "their way" is the best approach for everyone. They don't know quite where to go with these insights, but commit to exploring them further, maybe even with outside help.

Once Social Changers' members have completed an exploration of their internal patterns, their leader intends to focus attention on how they interact with groups and organizations in the community. She knows that there are some strained relationships and wonders if a better understanding of their internal dynamics will provide insights about their organizational projections. She sees the staff conversation that focused on the *Exclusivity* shadow as an opening.

Three further examples

In order to expand the reader's understanding of the Strengths and Shadows Model we have included three additional graphic depictions of organizational culture. Each one was developed in a different way.

The Save Our Youth graphic (see Figure 8.2) was the result of a group of researchers finding patterns as they reviewed the data from a research project on the organization. The graphic was their chosen way to present the information to the organization's leaders. The graphic for 2V/ACT (see Figure 8.3) was created during a reflective learning discussion between graduate students and the organization's last executive director after the organization had been closed for a few years. The Connection's graphic (see Figure 8.4) was constructed in a staff retreat with all staff contributing to the organizational picture. Staff constructed the original graphic at one planning retreat and then updated it four years later.

Figure 8.2. Save Our Youth

Save Our Youth is an organization devoted to making life better for street-involved and other at-risk youth. Its graphic depicts how in general the empathic nature of the organization's work is connected to the stress felt by staff, but it also shows how working with at-risk street youth created specific Strengths and Shadows. One example is the Strength of *Empathy* and the Shadow of *Blurred Boundaries*. In addition the graphic demonstrates the interconnectedness of various cultural elements. Two Strengths can have the same Shadow; for example, *Hopeful* and *Commitment to Mission* both have the Shadow of *Despair*. This interconnection shows a certain tenacity of the cultural elements and also points to opportunities to leverage change.

Figure 8.3. 2V/ACT

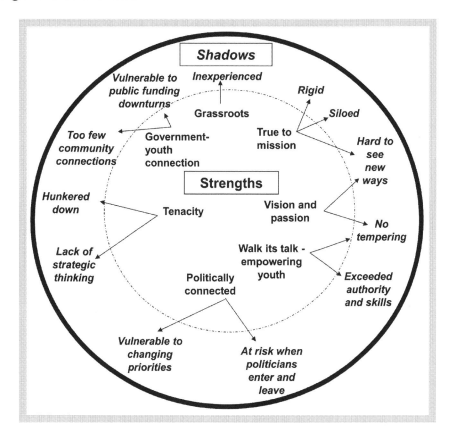

Though also a youth-involving/serving organization, 2V/ACT's purpose was to empower and support youth to participate in their community's civic and political processes. Its graphic depicts different aspects of serving a youth population. For example, there is no indication of despair related to this organization's work with youth, but there is evidence that a "youth culture" influenced the organization. The Strength of Empowering Youth created Shadows of *Exceeded Authority and Skills* and *No Tempering of Actions*. The 2V/ACT graphic also illustrates how the work style of an organization, in this case its close ties to government and political connections, affected its culture and made it vulnerable to changing politics.

Figure 8.4. Connections

Connections is an agency serving victims of sexual and domestic violence and general crimes as well as homeless individuals and families. Its graphic shows a sophisticated understanding of organizational patterns by the staff who developed it. That sophistication partially results from their having used this tool multiple times to understand their organization's culture. The depth of their understanding also comes from their leader's commitment to creating learning opportunities for herself and her staff. The complexity of the insights and intensity of some of the wording are reminders of the alive and dynamic nature of an organization's culture and a staff's experience of it. In the Save Our Youth graphic the Shadows of *Overwork, Lack of Self-Care, Burnout* and *Feelings of Despair* come from the Strength of *Commitment and Empathy for Each Youth*. In the Connections graphic the Shadows of *Overextended, Burned Out and Hopeless*, and *Depressed* come from *Commitment to Ending DV-SA-Homelessness*, rather than work with individual clients. This contrast suggests different organizational dynamics at work and perhaps indicates a different approach to addressing desired changes.

As shown in these three examples, some themes occur across organizations. For example, "Mission" appears on each graphic though its wording as a Strength, and its accompanying Shadows are unique to each entity. On the other hand some Strengths appear on just one organization's graphic. They are distinctive characteristics of that culture, for example, Connection's *"Tude"* and 2V/ACT's *"Government-Youth Connection"*.

In order to avoid the pitfalls of traumatization and to help an organization thrive, its members need to be able to recognize and explore its culture. As a key internal resource person, the leader's role in supporting this organizational learning and renewal is crucial. She or he sets the stage and models the kind of openness necessary for this work to succeed. A consultant might also be helpful to organizational learning. The consultant's role, as an external resource person, brings an important complementary perspective to the organization's learning efforts. In the next two chapters we explore in detail the ways these two roles help organizations heal, recover, and improve their health and sustainability.

9

LEADING IN TIMES OF ORGANIZATIONAL TRAUMA

Leaders are critical in helping to heal traumatized organizations. While they cannot always protect an organization from trauma, leaders can help protect the organizational culture from traumatization. Their interpretation of events as well as their approach and actions strongly influence the dynamics within their organizational cultures. A leader's approach may be a mitigating factor, promoting healing within the organizational culture, or it may exacerbate the negative impacts of the situation and potentially threaten the future of the system.

This chapter describes the role of leaders in traumatization recovery. Two stories that exemplify the concepts are included. These stories come from Shana's research on leading during organizational trauma (Hormann, 2007). One story is about a leader who came into an agency after trauma occurred and facilitated the organization's recovery from traumatization. The second story is about a leader who led her organization during organizational trauma and through the process of healing. Both stories were updated four years after the initial study, allowing the leaders to reflect on their experiences and comment on the long-term impact of their interventions.

Leadership Functions

Leaders are called on to provide multiple functions in circumstances of trauma and traumatization (See Table 9.1). They are key to identifying that the system is suffering, naming that suffering, and recognizing that the organization is a traumatized system. Once recognition and naming has occurred, leaders are essential for containing the impacts of traumatization and offering their optimism, confidence, and energy to the recovery and healing processes. They are necessary champions of the organizational strengths and help staff to keep these strengths in mind. Leaders also provide multiple frameworks for helping organizational members make sense of what is happening and make decisions about how to move forward. By being knowledgeable about what might occur during and after trauma and what they might be called on to provide in their leadership role, leaders can be prepared and more confident about their abilities to handle turbulent and stressful organizational dynamics in a healthy and productive manner. Table 9.1 summarizes a leader's role and its impact.

Identify suffering and name organizational traumatization

Leaders need to be attentive to organizational patterns to recognize widespread suffering when it occurs. In order to see traumatization as a possibility, leaders need to learn about organizational trauma and be able to recognize its characteristics. They can then name the situation for what they believe it to be – "We have experienced a trauma" or "We are a traumatized organization." Correctly identifying trauma and traumatization sets the stage for effective intervention.

Contain impacts of traumatization

In order to effectively assist their organizations, leaders need to be aware of their own history, predispositions, strengths and shortcomings. If they do not understand their own patterns and behaviors, they run the risk of being influenced unconsciously by blind spots in their thinking or being triggered by their own experiences and memories. Or they might be unduly surprised by staff's reactions and unable to focus on events and circumstances taking place. The more self-aware leaders are, the more confidently they can act and the clearer their vision and guidance can be.

When they know themselves well, leaders can be centers of calm and act as containers for surfacing suppressed dynamics and feelings. They can be prepared for stress, turmoil, reactivity, and emotional contagion that arise in a traumatized system. With unwavering purpose and emotional stability they can act in a non-anxious manner, especially important in unstable situations. Leaders who are consistent and calm help reduce fear and anxiety in their organizations.

Table 9.1. Leadership Functions and Impact

Leadership Functions	Professional Development	Organizational Impact
Identify suffering and name organizational traumatization	Learn about organizational trauma and traumatization	Deterioration of the situation stops
Contain impacts of traumatization	Be aware of own history, strengths, and blind spots	Less organizational anxiety, confusion, and helplessness
Offer optimism, confidence, and energy	Develop non-blaming dialogue skills and a non-anxious presence	More positive interactions and less negative emotional contagion
Provide frameworks for analysis and meaning making	Learn about organizational culture and lifecycles	Collective understanding of individuals and system
Champion organizational strengths	Become familiar with a strengths-based approach	More organizational confidence and optimism
Model kindness, compassion, and healthy boundaries	Practice caring strategies and mindfulness techniques and learn about compassion fatigue	Less blame, more productivity, renewed relationships with external environment
Ask for outside help when necessary	Address perceptions of success and vulnerability	More hope, energy, and confidence

Offer optimism, confidence, and energy

Leaders' optimism, confidence, and energy, which come from their own personal and professional development practices, help them and the organization as a whole stay with the process of learning even in challenging times. They act from the belief that organizational learning comes from ongoing discovery and conversation. Leaders model and provide arenas to share hope, energy, and spirit and encourage staff members to build a collective optimism for positive change. They model non-blaming dialogue throughout the process and reinforce collective responsibility rather than individual scapegoating. Increased positive interactions contain and decrease negative emotional contagion.

Provide frameworks for analysis and meaning making

By articulating in everyday language their understanding of the organization's status and by asking probing questions to promote collective meaning making, leaders help others to understand the organizational culture and experience. Meaning making is especially powerful when leaders create forums for organizational members to hear each other's thinking about what has occurred. Staff are better able to see how their individual experiences and feelings fit into and make up the larger organizational picture. Storytelling can also illuminate the current organizational narrative and patterns of behavior, heretofore unconscious or hidden, and may provide clues about helpful interventions.

Champion organizational strengths

Storytelling is an opportunity for leaders and their staff to remember and appreciate organizational strengths. Using the Strengths and Shadows Model helps the organization catalogue its strengths in a systematic way. In situations of trauma and during its aftermath these strengths may be forgotten – or only their shadows be noticed – with a resulting feeling of helplessness. Leaders can remind organizational members about the strengths and how they could be used to move forward.

Model kindness, compassion, and healthy boundaries

Times of sharing are important occasions for individuals across the system to be together. Shared stories and feelings allow organizational members to develop a collective sense of concern for one another and for the group as a whole. Leaders can model kindness and care while emphasizing stories that hold themes of compassion and hope.

During all interactions including collective storytelling, supervision sessions, and one-to-one conversations leaders can help members focus on their organization rather than on individuals. Consistent focus on systemic patterns and collective responsibility mitigate blame and scapegoating of one person or one group, allowing the organizational culture to heal.

Once organizational members have paid attention to their internal dynamics and accepted ownership of internal patterns the leaders can help the organization reconsider its relationships with the community. The leaders can model approaching other groups and agencies with a spirit of openness rather than hypervigilance.

Ask for outside help when necessary

When leaders reach out for assistance, traumatized organizations can benefit from feedback and infusion of energy from the external environment. Leaders' individual learning and self-awareness help them recognize their own and their organization's limits and give them confidence to ask for outside help when necessary. Outside help is useful in several situations. For example, outside help is very important when a leader is unable to maintain a non-anxious approach. The leader may be personally overwhelmed by the trauma itself or the intensity of the situation she faces. A consultant or peer who is not caught up in the events and emotions can help mitigate organizational and leadership anxiety and support a calm and thoughtful approach. Outside support may include individual coaching with a leader in preparation for work with the whole system. In a related circumstance a leader may struggle to name strengths, even going so far as to think the organization is just living in the shadows. Secondly, a leader might not be able to separate out his patterns from organizational patterns. In both of these situations, feedback from a source external to the system can help the leader identify her or his individual patterns as well as organizational patterns. Thirdly, outside help may be needed when organizational members, including the leader, are grieving. Someone not impacted by the loss is needed to create an opportunity for members to acknowledge and mourn. This need is especially important in organizations where the pattern is to skip over the grief and get on with the work.

Two Accounts of Trauma and Healing from the Leaders' Perspectives

The accounts of trauma and healing in this section are from two nonprofit organizations. One nonprofit is in a large urban area, predominantly serving one city, and the second is in a large rural area. In the first story the leader joined the organization after it had become a traumatized system, and in the second the leader was present during the trauma and resulting traumatization.

The first story describes how one leader: 1) acted as a non-anxious presence and worked to contain traumatization within an organization, 2) engaged her staff teams in healing by increasing positive interactions and focusing on organizational strengths, 3) made use of outside help, and, 4) "held" the organization by modeling compassion and healthy boundaries.

Cora's story

Cora came into a traumatized system as an interim director in 1999 and was hired as the permanent executive director the next year. The agency she directed is located in a large urban area. She told her story to Shana in 2006 with additional comments added in 2011.

As interim director Cora met Pat who had been hired by the board of directors to conduct an organizational survey of the agency in concert with hiring a new executive director. Board and staff identified the qualities of hard work, dedication, and commitment as organizational characteristics; however, one third of them also described a culture of crisis, "catastrophizing", and reactivity. Pat concluded that the agency was a traumatized system due to the cumulative effects of the work as well as cycles of organizational crises. Cora took advantage of the fact that the board of directors had sought outside help prior to her being hired. She had Pat's analysis of the organization's functioning to use as reference.

Prior to her role as interim director Cora had years of experience as an accountant with the private sector and a short number of years with the YWCA. Cora thought herself to be a competent, forthright, self-confident person who was good at listening to others and at following her own inner compass. Pat and Shana thought Cora to be a credible and capable professional; her demeanor was "crisp" although not edgy.

Cora reported the following: She entered the system and quickly discerned that there was a tremendous buildup of fear and anxiety among staff. Several staff reported that they suffered from secondary traumatic stress. She thought staff and board members' perceptions of each other and the agency were distorted, and that this high level of reactivity seemed normal to the members. Overall a depressed atmosphere pervaded the agency. She could see the dynamics without the history of being a part of them and was perceived by staff, board, and community members as separate from – and therefore not tainted by – those dynamics.

Cora quickly took steps to identify and contain the traumatization. First, she read Pat's report and learned the agency was described as "a traumatized system, experiencing the cumulative effects of the work itself and its cycles of crises." She also learned about the characteristics of a traumatized system including stress contagion and an exhausted organizational culture, with high turnover and inconsistent performance of executive directors and staff.

Second, Cora listened to staff, heard their perceptions, and learned about secondary trauma. She believed staff were capable workers and committed to providing services; however several of them were suffering from secondary traumatic stress and needed support. She brought her newfound understanding of trauma reactions at the individual and team levels to the board of directors, helped them to understand impacts on staff, and advocated for appropriate services to assist with healing.

Cora reported that when she began working at the agency the divisions between staff groups were obvious. Staff offices were grouped in a way that reinforced who was talking with whom; there was little contact from one side of the hall to the other. Cora purposefully set about to help the teams strengthen meaningful connections. She firmly encouraged relationships beyond the boundaries of established sub-groups by working with staff to rearrange office spaces and then assigning tasks across the sub-groups.

In addition, Cora used already existing structures and rituals to promote healing among the teams. For example, staff regularly took informal opportunities to meet and talk, including sitting down to have lunch together. She built upon that practice by introducing new ground rules, establishing lunch meetings during which all staff attended, and members were free to talk about anything. Slowly Cora and the staff built a safe environment. She reported that these actions taken together stopped "the revolving door" of staff being hired, trained, and then quitting. Subsequent staff joined the agency and stayed for a number of years. These times of sharing combined with more formal client consultation sessions facilitated the agency's becoming a learning organization, a system in which members took the time to reflect on what they were learning and how they were operating as a whole.

A system's learning about itself is not always an easy or smooth process. Cora shared the following story from her early years at the agency. She believed the story to be important as it highlighted the organization's ability to hold conflicting values and opinions and demonstrated healthy diversity of thought and approaches among staff:

Several staff approached Cora and told her they wanted her to publicly state that she was a feminist and the agency was a feminist organization. Her response was, "I'm a humanist not a feminist." She explained the word "feminist" had a negative connotation for her and so would not call herself one. A couple of staff members argued with her, telling her she was wrong. This internal agency conflict went on for some time. Cora maintained a calm and firm demeanor throughout this period although she admitted that she felt victimized by certain staff members who persisted in talking with her about this subject; they told her she was a feminist and pressured her to use the label. Cora learned about feminism from a number of sources and told staff members that she had learned positive attributes associated with feminism and was grateful for the learning. However, she continued to believe that she was not a feminist, and told her team that staff members did not have to think alike, she respected everyone, and she felt honored to work with them. Cora told Shana that in her experience there was strong emotion among staff members connected to each issue, positive and negative. She worked hard to de-escalate the strong negative emotions and build bridges with staff rather than meet their high levels of emotion with strong emotion of her own.

Throughout Cora's time with the agency she used the report Pat had prepared, referring to various sections and considering the health of the organization as compared to the time when the report was written. For example, she realized that secondary traumatic stress was an ongoing issue that needed attention. One response to this realization was to bring Pat and Shana into the organization to do a workshop for staff on organizational trauma and secondary trauma.

When Cora stopped to reflect at the end of her first two years with the organization, she identified an area of growth for herself. She had a tendency to rescue or fix situations and people, and she took on leading an agency that needed to be fixed! One way she could rescue was to answer the crisis line while staff members were involved in direct service with clients. Cora provided this service late into the evening after working all day. Her over-functioning was paid back by the joy that she felt from helping the staff. However, after a couple of months of answering the phones Cora realized she could not continue this behavior, the payoff of good feelings was not enough to balance the resulting stress and exhaustion of over-functioning. She chose instead to set and hold healthy boundaries at work by stopping this practice. She modeled what she believed was appropriate for the organization.

Finally, Cora emphasized to her staff that she was not the only leader in the agency, everyone had leadership capacity, and other staff members expressed leadership at different times. She told them often,

> No one of us can be the face of this agency. We always
> have to be educating each other.

Cora encouraged cross-training of staff and had staff members attend community meetings with her. Her approach empowered individuals and encouraged a spirit of cooperation and collaboration within the organization. Her approach also ensured that staff members built bridges between the organization and the external environment in addition to the ones she constructed and maintained.

Dee's story

This second description of leading during organizational trauma and traumatization illustrates how one leader navigated through organizational trauma without the benefit of knowing about traumatization and recovery within organizational cultures, and without the benefit of skilled outside help. This leader's commitment to the mission helped see the agency through a bleak and chaotic chapter. This leader: 1) recognized that the system was suffering, 2) shared her own energy with her team, 3) engaged her staff team in healing through outreach efforts, and, 4) and championed the organization's strengths, especially the agency's high-quality delivery of service.

Dee was hired as a counselor in 1998 at a rural agency that provided services to victims of domestic and sexual violence and their families. At the time of her hire the organization had a poor reputation, and few people were seeking services. As a long-time community member, Dee believed the services provided were essential.

The former executive director abruptly quit two months after Dee started working as a counselor, and Dee was asked by the board of directors to step into a leadership role. Dee described her predecessor as an emotionally abusive supervisor who threatened staff members about losing their jobs and publicly embarrassed them. Within days of Dee's assuming leadership funders froze the agency's grant money because the former executive director informed them, after she quit, that the agency was not in compliance with regulations. Dee and the board of directors had to lay off staff, and Dee remained the only paid employee for several months. She rebuilt relationships with the community and funders through meetings about programming and meticulous attention to financial detail. She subsequently rehired staff, insisted on careful documentation of services, and improved service capacity.

Dee thought the former director's actions – negative behavior toward staff and lack of accountability with funding sources – weakened the organization. However, it was ongoing subtle threats and overt hostility from local communities towards the organization that resulted in organizational traumatization. She believed the hostility was directed towards the organization's mission and work. As an example Dee shared the following story about the role of the organization in supporting and advocating for a teenage victim of sexual assault:

A thirteen-year-old girl was sexually assaulted by an adult man. Dee's agency provided support and legal advocacy services for the young victim through the legal process and the trial. Staff members assumed the man would be found guilty of statutory rape given the age difference between the parties involved. Dee and other staff members were stunned by the jury's verdict of "not guilty." She described the organizational culture as depressed immediately afterward; a sense of powerlessness prevailed for a number of weeks. Dee felt hurt and angry on behalf of the young woman because of the jury verdict. Adding to the organizational stress, the young victim, needing support, was in the office daily during and after the trial. Given the small size of the agency and the myriad of personal and professional connections in the county, staff never had respite from the situation.

Dee and her team spent hours sharing stories about the trial and their ongoing interactions with community members. They also talked about actions they could take in response to the verdict but repeatedly came back to the disappointing conclusion that any public response they might make as an agency could rebound negatively on the young victim. Dee believed their sharing together was useful for support among team members. However, it also reinforced the team's sense of powerlessness. After a number of weeks staff finally refocused their energy and action on serving victims and their families. Staff also felt an urgency about increasing their community education efforts and began planning how to do so.

Given the negative and sometimes hostile interactions between the agency and community members, both during and after the trial, Dee knew she had to establish, maintain, and strengthen bridges from the organization to the external environment. One such bridge was hosting breakfasts for law enforcement officials, judges, and prosecuting attorneys to create venues for interaction with community members.

These gatherings allowed for relationship building and sharing areas of common interest.

When Dee reflected on the trial and its outcome, she realized engagement with the wider community was important for the agency's health. Because of the agency's poor relationships with the community, the impetus to close organizational boundaries was strong. However, Dee, staff, and board members knew the importance of keeping the lines of communication open. In the years since this court case community support has grown and services have expanded.

Dee also reflected on her tendency to get overly attached to individuals and overly attached to outcomes. She said she sometimes had unrealistic expectations and then felt depressed when her expectations were not met. She added:

> I need to keep close attention to what I'm telling myself.
> If I'm not acutely listening to what's happening inside,
> I come to conclusions without even knowing that I am
> doing it.

Dee believed if she were more aware of her assumptions and self-talk she would recognize quickly when her expectations were unrealistic. She was more vulnerable to missing cues and to judging herself and others harshly when she was exhausted and neglecting her spiritual practice.

Final comments

These two women were dependable, trustworthy, and supportive, qualities that were essential to their being credible leaders and helping their organizations through very difficult times. Here is a summary of each of their stories from the perspective of leadership functions.

Cora learned about organizational trauma from an assessment written about the agency prior to her joining it. She immediately began addressing issues to contain the impacts of organizational traumatization. For example, she worked with and listened to clinical staff members who identified the prevalence of secondary trauma among the therapists. In response Cora asked a staff member to explain secondary trauma to her board members and then worked with the board to secure needed resources for staff. Her actions helped reduce organizational anxiety. She also brought optimism, confidence, and energy to her role, and her non-anxious presence minimized negative emotional contagion. This approach worked well in a culture with strong emotion among staff members about their work and about issues related to feminism and violence against women. She was frequently able to de-escalate situations and contribute to an organizational culture that could accept different perspectives and avoid individual blame.

Dee joined an agency that was in crisis due to actions by the previous executive director; the crisis covered up ongoing hostility between the agency and its environment. Once Dee resolved issues related to agency functioning, community hostility towards the agency and the resulting traumatization became apparent. Dee was overwhelmed by the extent of the community hostility. In addition she was emotionally hooked by her relationship with the young victim and her feelings about the trial's outcome. Dee, because of her own feelings, was unable to contain the traumatization and help staff make sense of the situation. Staff and Dee closed ranks and turned inward. They lost focus on wider issues and needs of families and victims. Eventually Dee began to strategize about how best to move her staff and agency forward. She turned her energy outward and reinforced connections with the community rather than protection of the agency. Over time she became more aware of her own patterns and their effect on the organization. Under her leadership the agency grew in effectiveness and strengthened its standing in the county.

This chapter described the role of leaders in traumatization recovery and clarified leadership concepts. The two stories illustrated the leaders' actions during and immediately following organizational traumatization. One of the stories illustrated how a leader benefited from resources offered by a consultant skilled in organizational traumatization identification and intervention. The next chapter describes the role of the consultant more fully.

10

CONSULTING TO TRAUMATIZED SYSTEMS

External consultants play a highly useful role in helping organizations through the painful experiences of trauma. They work in the immediate aftermath to help an organization recover and heal, and they assist an organization make sense of experiences and cope with harmful dynamics after the discovery of trauma. As an external resource person not directly harmed by the trauma, a consultant can offer structure and approaches that support and empower the organization and its members. This chapter focuses on the role of consultant, including foundational concepts of consulting and components that help someone in the role succeed. Building on the fundamentals of collaborative consultation, we explore what it takes to consult with organizations suffering from trauma and traumatization.

We begin this chapter with a story about a partnership between Pat in her external consultant role and an organization's leader and how that partnership helped an organization cope with trauma during a critical time in its existence.

The Connections Story

In 2007 Kate, director of the Connections Program, called Pat for help. She was reeling from a major meltdown that had occurred at a staff retreat a month earlier. The surface trigger involved a conversation about a changed phone greeting necessitated by a new contract, but the judgments, vehemence, pain, and hurt from that discussion suggested deeper issues were at work. In heated exchanges staff accused each other of straying from the organization's true mission by taking any money offered, of rejecting new ideas, of ignoring new staff. A split between longer-term and newer staff was emerging. Kate personally felt overwhelmed and stunned by the depth of emotion and lack of empathy in the exchanges. She and her staff had successfully weathered crises before, but this seemed different, more intense. She remembered all too well the case study Pat and Shana had written about the demise of a rape crisis agency. Kate knew she and Connections needed help. She did not want these negative internal dynamics to damage the program and threaten its existence. Kate felt confident that with help she and her staff could weather the situation. The situation was troubling, but Kate had no idea that this was only the beginning of two years of turmoil for her organization.

A little background: Kate Rowe-Maloret was the director of Connections, a program that provided services to homeless people and victims of domestic violence, sexual assault, and general crimes. Kate met Pat in 2000 when she was participating in a statewide advisory committee. Pat met other Connections staff during a trip to their county in 2002. Kate later asked Pat to consult with them on Connections' strategic planning efforts.

Pat became increasingly familiar with the program, its staff, and its community during the course of that planning project. She and Kate developed a mutually trusting relationship, and after the project was completed, they kept in touch with each other about Connections' growth and challenges. Kate also became familiar with the research and writing Pat and Shana were doing on organizational trauma and healing.

When Kate called Pat in 2007, they talked about the issues from the retreat, the quality of relationships among the staff, and the need for Connections to revisit and renew its strategic plan. The wider environment was changing too rapidly for the Connections staff to be caught up in negative internal dynamics. Together Pat and Kate decided an all-day session offered the opportunity for staff to clear the air and make sense of what was going on. A date was chosen, all staff agreed to participate, and Pat interviewed each staff person by phone beforehand.

The retreat day arrived, and both Pat and Kate were nervous. This was an opportunity for staff to really communicate with each other and move on, but the pitfalls were clear. Emotions could rip open wounds from the earlier retreat. Individuals could refuse to engage. Pat proposed an approach that supported reflection, personal responsibility, and compassionate inquiry rather than debate.

From conversation in pairs to full group dialogue, the staff began to engage with each other. One key moment shifted the tenor of the conversation. A staff person burst into tears as she tried to share what she was experiencing. With some support from Pat she shared her feelings honestly. Invited by Pat, each of her colleagues responded to her. That honest sharing of pain and dismay and compassionate listening shifted the energy in the room. Some important truths emerged. With further reflection the staff created a set of norms to support their work with each other. Other exercises allowed the staff to see their collective development over the past few years, to understand how their work was affecting their internal atmosphere, and to recognize their collective strengths. They began to rebuild their sense of care for each other and agreed on ways to support that rebuilding. They were not finished, but they had started healing their relationships. They ended the day with identification of strategic planning items.

Pat and Kate acknowledged the gains of the day and agreed to begin a strategic planning process sometime the next spring. But that spring Connections staff began hearing word about big changes. Their parent agency was merging operations with a mental health agency in the next county, and Connections would be folded into that other agency's programs. No officials were communicating with Connections staff about this decision, so it came as a complete surprise to Kate and her staff. No staff knew what would happen to them or the services they provided. The core identity and existence of this locally-based community program was being threatened. Staff were outraged at this decision, and on an emotional level felt awful: helpless, abandoned, disrespected, and unvalued. Staff and Kate were left reeling from the implications of this decision. This change might mean the end of their program. This decision traumatized Connections. Kate realized she had to fight this action; she could not let the change happen because it threatened services in their home county. "I had to act on behalf of our agency and the people we serve." Despite a context of uncertainty, Kate was determined to get through the situation. She also admitted to being a little naïve about what she was in for.

State agency grantors decided this move across county lines could not occur without significant renegotiation of contracts in effect, and those renegotiations seemed very unlikely to succeed. Amidst complicated administrative and financial pressures, Connections staff put aside strategic planning and attempted to discuss rationally different scenarios for their future. They were trying their best to see their way through this turbulent and lonely time.

No one inside Connections had ultimate say about what would happen to their program or to their jobs. The county commissioners would determine if Connections would be allowed to stay a county program or they would let it go. That fall the commissioners agreed the county would temporarily administer Connections, but they would take another five months – until the winter of the following year – to make a final decision. In the meantime unanswered questions of cash flow and financial management issues hung over the county and the program. This extended period of waiting intensified organizational insecurity and staff feelings of anxiety.

Connections staff carried on providing services day to day during this extremely stressful and uncertain time. Another consultant working with the county and the program commented:

Staff steadfastly served county residents despite uncertainty about the future of their continuing employment, and all deserved the gratitude of the community and recognition of how difficult this transition period [was].

Kate provided critical leadership in taking on new administrative responsibilities and managing the relationship with the county as well as providing ways for staff to support each other. Pat stayed in touch with Kate and heard how she and staff were handling the uncertainty and pressure. Pat thought that the work staff had accomplished at the 2007 session gave them a foundation to cope collectively with this traumatic situation. They had rebuilt sufficient trust in one another so they could utilize their organizational strengths to survive.

In February 2009, the county commissioners decided to keep Connections as a county program. Connections staff felt instant relief and some disbelief. Everyone had been worried that Kate would resign and the program would fold, though interestingly, Kate had thrived on the challenge and said, "Just watch me!" The traumatizing uncertainty was over, but staff were still feeling its impact. And they still had not completed their strategic plan. What did they need to do to put this traumatic year behind them, to return to their own agenda, and to create the program's future?

Kate and Pat talked once more and decided on another full day session. That session would be a time to acknowledge what they had been through and set the stage for strategic planning. It was a day to vent, validate, and shift gears. Pat's role was to support them by structuring their time and holding a safe and healthy environment for emotional expression and responses. Amidst tears and laughter staff took the opportunity to voice out loud how scared they had been that they were going to lose their leader. Some had agonized privately about seeking other jobs if their livelihoods were in danger, and many revealed their fears that Connections itself might fold. Staff shared honestly and listened compassionately. They were ready to move on.

Later that spring staff embarked on a strategic planning process and met in a retreat setting to forge their future. Building on current efforts and opening up new directions left staff energized about innovative possibilities for Connections.

About a year later Kate brought Pat up to date about how things were going, and they took time to reflect together on all that had happened. Staff relationships continued to be healthy with direct communication on issues related to burnout and coping. With some staff restructuring Connections was stable and taking on new challenges. Staff members were thriving with additional responsibilities and had made amazing progress in advancing program work.

What learning did Kate and Pat draw from this set of experiences?

The nature of the meltdown in 2007 threatened Connections at its core. Staff's usual assertive attitude and feistiness toward outsiders (an important element of their advocacy) was turned inward on each other. While arguing about the meaning of social change and Connections' mission, some staff trivialized others' pain and stopped listening to each other, ultimately threatening the basis of their relationships and their work. Kate had seen earlier dynamics similar to these and knew how damaging they could be for the organization. She did not want to lose good people. Her own joy in the work felt threatened. Kate felt too "drawn" in to provide a healthy container for the conflict and to be neutral in any discussion to address the dynamics.

However, Kate was a wise leader. Her insight about her own limitations and her knowledge of organizational trauma led her to ask for help at that critical moment in 2007. She felt confident enough in her role to make this move, even though it was a hard thing to do. The long-standing relationship and trust between Kate and Pat helped. Getting assistance at this critical juncture enabled Connections to heal its internal relationships and (unknowingly) gird itself for the turmoil still to come. Kate never lost sight of a positive outcome, and Pat brought her hope and optimism to the effort.

Having shared this story, we turn now to our thinking about the role of consultant in helping traumatized systems.

Conceptual Foundation of Consulting

Four practitioners provided the conceptual foundation of consulting with traumatized organizations, and our own organizational work and the experiences of colleagues deepened that foundation. Peter Block (2000), a seminal thinker in organization development, described how to succeed in work with clients by using a collaborative consulting approach. Howard F. Stein, whose practice is in psychoanalytic anthropology, explored the cultural unconscious and its pervasive influence on organizational functioning (1987, 2004). Anton Obholzer and Vega Zagier Roberts investigated unconscious sources of stress in human service organizations and developed productive ways to work with staff of those organizations (1994).

A collaborative approach offers the most effective partnership for change (Block, 2000). Client and consultant join together to take advantage of the knowledge and perspective each brings to the situation. Success rests on relationships, and those relationships depend on authentic interactions between consultant and client. Problem solving tasks – focused on the content of the issue at hand and what to do about it – operate at one level of the consulting process. Attention to feelings, building trust, noticing expressed and unexpressed needs, and being present and responsible all operate at a second level. Authenticity is key to succeeding at this second level. By integrating both levels of work the consultant can partner with the client organization to achieve the desired change.

Stein takes consulting further by seeking to unearth what is beneath the "crust" of culture (2004) in order to more fully understand an organization's reality. Using a psychodynamic perspective, he maps contradictions between the espoused story of the culture and the organization's unconscious processes and hidden dimensions. This mapping allows a deeper analysis of the situation and a more compassionate connection to all individuals working within an organization. Ultimately Stein offers a practice framework of:

> ...emotional inclusiveness in which the consultant
> becomes an advocate not for one leader, one member
> or one group but rather for the maturity and integrity
> of the whole system (Stein, 1987, p.364).

Obholzer and Roberts (1994) focus specifically on individual and organizational stress in human service organizations. They explore a variety of situations in which the unconscious dynamics of the work are little understood and almost completely unmanaged. Immersing themselves in powerful organizational undercurrents, they experienced firsthand the complex effects of these dynamics. They poignantly describe the impact of these consultations on the consultants themselves.

Block, Stein, Obholzer, and Roberts together offer a complex picture of the consulting process and a set of implications for the consultant's role. The consulting process is nonlinear, not a set of steps to follow. Delving into the unconscious and emotional life of groups and organizations is not for everyone. The next section focuses on skills, characteristics, and experiences that help consultants succeed in working with traumatized organizations.

Components of Consultant Success

What does it take to succeed in this work? We have grouped the answers into four categories:

- Emotional predisposition

- Professional approach

- Relevant experience and learning

- Skills

Emotional predisposition

Love for organizations and their people and a ready willingness to immerse oneself in the relational aspects of consulting are fundamental to consulting to traumatized systems. These dispositions are essential whether the work begins in the immediate aftermath of trauma or starts as an exploration of organizational culture or history.

A consultant needs be ready to listen to the client's story, establish rapport in an evenhanded way, and be prepared to lend a hand even if the situation sounds messy and stuck. The consultant's rapport-building capacity allows her to engage quickly. Relationship energy enables the consultant to show care and concern for organizational members and the organization as a whole. In these trying circumstances it is important for the consultant to demonstrate compassion for the difficulty of the situation and appreciation for the complex and often intractable dynamics that are occurring.

Client members might be scared, resistant, confused, angry, withdrawn, or completely discouraged. The consultant's willingness to stay open in these tender moments and to give members the benefit of the doubt is essential. The power of modeling this open and caring attitude is important in any consultant-client relationship, but it is critical when working inside traumatized systems. Pat's ongoing relationship with Kate and Connections staff enabled her to be authentically caring and compassionate. She had already demonstrated a sincere interest in the welfare of the staff and the program as a whole.

To do this work the consultants need their own sources of sustainable positive energy. Enthusiasm, good cheer, appropriate humor, flexibility, resilience, and optimism are important antidotes to the painful experiences and helpless feelings in the organization itself.

Taken together, these qualities bolster a consultant's capacity to provide hope and to offer a way through the situation for the client. For example, Pat's enthusiasm, enjoyment of groups, and trusting relationship with the staff and Kate enabled her to be optimistic and compassionate during many moments of discouragement and pain.

It is helpful for a consultant to have a personal discipline or practice to sustain his or her positive attitude. This discipline could be participation in prayer, meditation, walks in nature, or some other process of self-reflection and renewal. The discipline helps the consultant draw from a larger source of energy and see his or her work in a larger context. The consultant's energy and balance nurture the organization's spirit and support and encourage the organization's own processes of renewal and replenishment. A practitioner's willingness to be authentic and open about his or her own practice also gives permission for organizational members to pay attention to spiritual dimensions of their work and their organization

These qualities and practices help the consultant maintain good boundaries and a healthy detachment in the helping role. She or he can value the organization's purpose and individual members without becoming caught up dynamics. She can be motivated to help without relying on the organization for validation, and she can avoid falling into the trap of rescuing or saving the organization. When a consultant can be stable and centered in emotionally charged situations, she or he can help contain the organization's sense of being out of control. Because she acts with empathy to establish and nurture trusting relationships, she might be momentarily swept up in the client's dynamics. However, clear boundaries enable her to recognize when she is caught up in others' perceptions and emotions and to respond skillfully. The consultant can use those "immersion" experiences to understand the system while maintaining her own independent perspective. Pat's decades of consulting experience with nonprofits has helped her forge her own approach: caring nonattachment for organizations, ability to be blunt and kind, and sufficient comfort with others' emotional turmoil.

The consultant's own history, predispositions, traumas, and hardships influence her practice. Insights about these factors help the consultant separate her issues from client-system issues. No consultant can anticipate all of his or her triggers and address them ahead of time so disciplined reflective practice is central to self-awareness and self-management. This practice helps the consultant maintain integrity and stamina in her work. Pat's and Shana's long-term colleagueship and friendship have enabled them to challenge and deepen each other's insights, to build on each other's creativity, and to notice each other's reactivity in work with clients.

Professional approach

Traumatized systems are fraught with anxiety, fear, anger, heightened emotion, and uncertainty. A system with trauma in its history may exhibit a less-intense version of these feelings. The system will challenge the consultant to apply her intellectual resources in emotionally charged circumstances. Realistically, she needs to enjoy the experience of entering into these situations, because from the beginning she has to act as a non-anxious container for emotional expression and feelings of anxiety and despair. Her attitude – non-judgmental, calm, poised, graceful, hopeful – will encourage the organization's members to accept her guidance, take risks, and participate honestly.

Since the focus is organizational trauma and organizational culture, it is essential the consultant be grounded in a big-picture approach to organizational life. When consultants express love and compassion for the whole organization, they help members see the harm to the organization itself. With careful listening consultants can discern patterns and point them out in ways that enable members to see the complexity of their situation. Focus on the whole is important whether helping an organization recover from the immediate aftermath of trauma or enabling it to discover and face unhealed traumas of its past. For example, Pat had used the Strengths and Shadows Model to help Connections staff develop an understanding of their culture and their organizational patterns.

When working with leaders, the broad approach needs to be balanced with empathy for individuals. Leaders frequently feel at fault or blamed for what has transpired. They need special support for their pain so they can function effectively in any exploration or healing. The mutual trust Pat and Kate held for each other enabled Pat to be genuinely supportive of Kate during these turbulent times.

Lastly, it helps immensely if the consultant likes exploring less-obvious dynamics of organizational life, including unconscious and psychodynamic aspects of organizational culture. The consultant's knowledge of organizational culture can help group members unearth hidden dynamics. Her knowledge can also help members recognize inherent stress in their caring or social change work. The consultant's comfort with talking about "undiscussable" or undiscovered aspects of organizational life helps organizational members get to central issues and concerns. Versatility and open-mindedness in using multiple frames of understanding afford a consultant many ways to enter and comprehend a system. Using strengths and shadows as a starting place for systemic analysis offers one nonjudgmental way to start a conversation.

Relevant experience and learning

Further credibility comes from relevant experience and learning: working in or consulted with highly mission-driven nonprofits; belonging to a network of practitioners and other professional allies, and participating in a community of practice.

However gained, knowledge about the world of nonprofits and the nature of highly mission driven organizations is vital. It is important to understand the realities of nonprofit life and the challenges of keep-ing individual wants and organizational requirements, internal values and external expectations, and available resources and needs in bal-ance. It is also important to understand the impact of wider service delivery systems and social change movement dynamics on individual organizations.

An organizational culture framework, familiarity with typical dynam-ics and patterns in nonprofit organizations, and understanding normal nonprofit life cycles are useful. The consultant also needs to under-stand the psychologies of trauma, loss and grief as they relate to organizational life, be aware of criteria to recognize trauma risk and trauma history, and be conversant with sustainability perspectives related to nonprofits. These frameworks help consultant and organi-zational members discuss the nature and sources of the tensions and dilemmas. Are they related to individual challenges, interpersonal dynamics, or organizational patterns? Are they related to present cir-cumstances or unfinished business from the past? Are dynamics due to normal occurrences in the organization's life cycle, or are they better explained by organizational trauma?

It is important for a consultant to understand basic systems dynam-ics in order to see the whole organizational experience, and appre-ciate the range of perspectives held within an organization and its subsystems. Noticing organizational dynamics and patterns (not just personalities and interpersonal relationships), and recogniz-ing and affirming collective meaning-making assure focus stays on the organization as a system. Organizations, especially human ser-vices, tend to notice narrower issues and patterns, frequently those related to people and interpersonal dynamics. Consultants must rely on themselves to bring and hold the organizational perspective.

Since leaders are central to the life of an organization, understanding leadership and its role in healthy and unhealthy organizations is essen-tial. It is crucial that the consultant appreciate the pain and turmoil a leader goes through in a traumatic situation. Sufficient rapport between consultant and leader enables the leader to be vulnerable enough to explore his or her part in organizational processes and risk trying new behaviors. Kate's trust of Pat enabled her to ask for help, to be honest and vulnerable about her experiences, and to follow Pat's suggestions about team sessions.

Skills

Design, coaching, and facilitating skills are further refinements of the collaborative consultation approach. Design skills enable consultants to create structures and processes for client organizations to engage in work. These skills are critically important in circumstances of high emotion and turmoil. Design skills enable consultants to act confidently. The consultant offers a purposeful and planned approach to a specific situation. In order to do that the consultant needs to be able to assess the situation and the organization's readiness to change. Based on knowledge of organizational trauma and its symptoms, consultants ask good questions to uncover enough of the story to make a choice about their involvement. If the fit is compatible, the consultant is in a position to offer guidance to talk about what is occurring and to help normalize individual and collective responses to the circumstances. Design skills also enable the consultant to make mid-course corrections as new information or circumstances arise, such as occurred in the Connections story. When the timing is right, the consultant can help shift the emotional focus on past and present to a more cognitive look at organizational priorities and the future. Design skills enable the consultant and client to discuss the overall trajectory of the project and to notice when the organization no longer needs the consultant's presence or help.

Because of the importance of organizational leadership, consultation will always include coaching leaders. Leaders may be board members, executive directors, or managers. Coaching focuses on two dimensions, helping leaders see their patterns and issues as they relate to the trauma and helping them prepare to act effectively with others to address the dynamics and issues. Supporting leaders in their personal exploration enables them to recognize their own feelings about the trauma and become aware of their own need for healing. The consultant can assist or encourage leaders to engage in that healing process so they are ready to act in open and non-defensive ways. The Connections story emphasizes the benefits of a mutually trusting relationship between leader and consultant.

Consultants and leaders together can think through ways to convene and facilitate conversations about organizational patterns and dynamics. Consultants can coach leaders on how to remain open and non-defensive. They can help leaders anticipate possible difficulties in discussions and respond without blaming, fixing, deflecting, or reacting as victim. Leaders who have worked through their own issues can use their new self-awareness in service of discovering and addressing organizational patterns and making changes.

Effective facilitation is key to any consultant's work. However, in circumstances of organizational trauma, certain aspects take on additional importance. An attentive, caring, and calm demeanor is critical to helping organizational members normalize their feelings and reactions. This includes assisting individuals and groups to cope with stages and tasks of grief and mourning often associated with trauma. Throughout the Connections project Pat was called on to facilitate discussions in emotionally charged circumstances and help build enough safety for sharing to take place. Furthermore, by being nonjudgmental and modeling collaborative dialogue the consultant can help group members integrate their individual experiences and insights into a collective experience and meaning.

The consultant can support group members to bring up "undiscussables" and train them to deal with resulting nervousness and conflict in constructive ways. In order to do so the consultant needs to be comfortable facilitating in the midst of tension and be ready to improvise when she realizes participants are surprised and stuck when "undiscussables" surface.

Consultants can model effective ways for organizational members to participate by noticing and naming relationship issues or counterproductive dynamics in the discussions. They can also offer specific tools to help members approach their dialogue in new ways. At several points in the Connections consultation Pat intentionally managed conversations and asked questions to surface previously unacknowledged feelings and thoughts. In one session staff members used compassionate listening to hear each other. That enabled one staff person to share openly about her feelings for the first time. In another session Pat created an atmosphere in which staff were able to acknowledge just how terrified they had been about the possibility of Kate's leaving and the program folding.

Capacity building of nonprofits and organizational change strategies will be more effective if an organization has healed from its traumas. Both leaders and consultants are important to that healing process. Practitioners who are willing and able to take on the difficult work of helping nonprofits heal play a vital role in strengthening the whole nonprofit sector.

11

LOOKING BACK AND LOOKING AHEAD

We know from continuing conversations with our colleagues, clients, and students over the past ten years that descriptions in this book mirror your organizational experiences. We have worked with many traumatized organizations and seen the harm done to both the organizations as a whole and to their members. We have heard stories of leaders' guilt about their failures to address situations successfully and have heard painful accounts from many individuals of leaving organizations with feelings of personal failure in their efforts to make a difference. As we sought to understand the dynamics of organizational trauma, we quickly realized how easy it was to be swept up in devastating events and patterns that most people cannot understand or control and to be left feeling helpless. We hope this book has given you new ways to look at and think about your organizations and also given you information, confidence, and hope about new ways to act.

This book focuses on the organizational entity itself because we recognize the power of systems and the need to address the fundamental dynamics of organizational culture. That notion works against the more popular ideas about organizational leadership, health, and change. In our decades of work as practitioners and educators we have encountered a very strong tendency to look for problems and answers in individuals, that is, in the smallest units of a human system. That tendency has led to problem definitions of stress, burnout, ineffective management, and leadership shortcomings, all of which miss the collective nature of the problems and the need for collective approaches to addressing them. That tendency has also led to the kinds of experiences of failure and defeat people have shared with us.

Our organizational perspective is not a criticism of self-care and stress-management skills and expectations, nor does it absolve individuals from being stewards of their own trauma responses. There is a deep need in the world of highly mission-driven nonprofits for individual efforts to be strong and persistent. Our analysis also does not ignore the importance of leadership development and management skills for nonprofit leaders. Those too are essential for healthy and sustainable organizations. We believe that our organizational perspective adds a missing and needed dimension of understanding about organizations. If highly mission-driven nonprofits are to survive and thrive through increasingly difficult political and economic times, leaders need to be able to accurately access their organization's health. We want leaders and members alike to be able to see themselves as part of a larger organizational culture – and to be comforted by this realization – so they can participate in collective action rather than address worries and concerns in isolation.

We started our thinking and writing by recognizing insidious patterns of cumulative trauma and naming traumatized systems as we were trying to help those suffering organizations. Only our own step back from the specifics allowed us to see organizational trauma in its many forms. That step back also enabled us to recognize that not all organizations suffered to the same degree, that some seemed to fare better than others in response to their work or traumatic times. There is more exploration and research to be done about what protects an organization from the deleterious effects of its work. For example, on the west coast an organization exists to document the stories of Japanese Americans who were unjustly incarcerated in camps during World War II. Despite the gravity of the content, this organization thrives and holds an optimistic forward-looking attitude and approach. How has this organization flourished in its work?

Even within the familiar realm of highly mission-driven nonprofits organizational experiences differ. That fact made it important to us to address organizations at risk for trauma as well as those in the throes of trauma. We wanted nonprofits to be able to use this information preventively and proactively as well as responsively. We believe in the power of organizational self-knowledge and its consequent self-esteem in helping organizations survive tough times. The Connections story exemplifies this power.

Our efforts at focusing on prevention encourage an organizational-learning approach. Given the current realities of organizational stress and worries about scarcity in the nonprofit sector, this approach is not usual. However, if an organization cannot find ways to step back from its day-to-day tasks, it will miss the fundamental patterns at play and the critical questions to address.

We also heard that our work was applicable to a wider range of organizations than we focused on in this book. Individuals working in businesses and governments shared poignant examples of traumatization and its terrible aftermath. And, of course, other people reminded us of community and societal traumas, such as the Columbine High School massacre and shooting sprees in their own cities or towns that left communities outraged, saddened, and bereft. We do think our ideas are relevant to these organizations and see future research as a way to explore beyond the experiences of our practice.

Our thinking about organizational culture and the influence of an organization's work on its collective life is relevant to a wide variety of organizations. It is as germane to the culture of high-tech companies, the US military, long-lasting bureaucracies, and the environmental movement as it is to highly mission-driven nonprofits. The work-culture connection can help many organizational members normalize patterns within their systems and avoid the pitfall of seeing all problems as individual or interpersonal ones. We hope individuals in those organizations will be interested in applying these ideas to their organizations' cultures and dynamics.

We hope this book has given you more ways to see your organizations and ideas about how to use the collective power of human energy within your organizations and communities to envision healthier ways of accomplishing your missions. Take whatever pieces are most useful. Have conversations with colleagues inside your organizations and programs, and beyond them. Mold these ideas to fit your circumstances and needs, challenge them, and push the edges of thinking about these ideas. Contact us – we would love to hear your responses and stories.

INDEX

REFERENCES

Block, P. (2000). Flawless consulting: A guide to getting your expertise used. San Francisco: Jossey-Bass Pfeiffer.

Couto, R.A. (1989). Redemptive organizations and the politics of hope. Clinical Sociology Review, 7, 64-79.

Figley, C.R. (Ed.) (1995). Compassion fatigue: Coping with secondary traumatic stress disorder in those who treat the traumatized. Florence, KY: Brunner/Mazel.

Green, B. (1989) Speaking one's truth: Process consultation with a feminist nonprofit board of directors. Unpublished master's thesis, Leadership Institute of Seattle, Graduate Center for Applied Behavioral Sciences, City University, Bellevue, WA.

Herman, J. (1992). Trauma and recovery: The aftermath of violence – from domestic abuse to political terror. New York: Basic Books.

Hormann, S. and Vivian, P. (2004).Seattle Rape Relief: Organizational trauma, agency closure, and interventions that might have made a difference, unpublished manuscript.

Hormann, S. (2007) Organizational Trauma: A phenomenological study of leaders in traumatized organizations. Unpublished doctoral dissertation, Antioch University, Yellow Springs, OH.

Linc Project. http://www.lincproject.org/organizing/ profiles/wroc_.shtml

Obholzer, A. and Roberts, V. Z. ed. (1994). The unconscious at work. New York: Routledge.

Pearlman, L.A., and Saakvitne, K.W. (1995). Trauma and the therapist: Countertransference and vicarious traumatization in psychotherapy with incest survivors. New York: W.W. Norton and Company.

Schein, E.H. (1985). Organizational culture and leadership. San Francisco: Jossey-Bass.

Schein, E.H. (1992). Organizational culture and leadership (Second ed.). San Francisco: Jossey-Bass.

Seattle Counseling Service. http://www.seattlecounseling.org/index.html.

Seattle Counseling Service 40th Anniversary Video, YoYoStringsMedia.com, 2010.

Seattle Counseling Service Newsletter, July 2010, electronic publication.

Stein, H. (1987). Encompassing systems: Implications for citizen diplomacy, Journal of Humanistic Psychology, 27, 3, 364-384.

Stein, H. (2004). Beneath the crust of culture. Amsterdam: Rodopi B.V.

Vivian, P. (2000). Nonprofit Assistance Center Organizational Assessment and Recommendations for Welfare Rights Organizing Coalition, unpublished report, 11.17.2000, p.2.

ABOUT THE AUTHORS

Pat Vivian, M.A., has consulted with hundreds of nonprofit and government organizations around the country for over 30 years. In her practice she has helped community-based agencies heal from organizational trauma and regain their health and effectiveness. She is a co-founder of the Community Consulting Partnership, which provides pro bono consulting to community-based nonprofits.

Shana Hormann, Ph.D., MSW, is a faculty member in the Organizational Development program at Antioch University Seattle. She has led and consulted with nonprofit, business, tribal, and government organizations for over 30 years. She has facilitated and supported organization and community change, diversity initiatives, leadership and team development, and conflict management.

Pat and Shana can be reached at vivianhormann@gmail.com

Made in the USA
Charleston, SC
01 April 2013